Anchors against Change

Anchors against Change

American Opinion Leaders' Beliefs
After the Cold War

Shoon Kathleen Murray

Ann Arbor
THE UNIVERSITY OF MICHIGAN PRESS

Copyright © by the University of Michigan 1996
All rights reserved
Published in the United States of America by
The University of Michigan Press
Manufactured in the United States of America
♾ Printed on acid-free paper

1999   1998   1997   1996   4   3   2   1

A CIP catalog record for this book is available from the British Library.

Library of Congress Cataloging-in-Publication Data

Murray, Shoon Kathleen, 1961–
     Anchors against change : American opinion leaders' beliefs after
the Cold War / Shoon Kathleen Murray.
        p.   cm.
     Includes bibliographical references and index.
     ISBN 0-472-10758-5 (cloth : acid-free paper)
     1. United States—Foreign relations—1989– —Public opinion.
     2. United States—Foreign relations—1945–1989—Public opinion.
     3. Cold War—Public opinion.   4. Public opinion—United States.
     I. Title.
     E840.M88   1996
     327.73—dc20   96-25342
                                                                  CIP

To my parents, Susan Colson and Keith Murray
my step-parents, David Colson and Lynne Fagan
and my brother, Tad Murray

Contents

Figures

Tables

Acknowledgments

Several people and organizations made it possible for me to create the Leadership Opinion Project (LOP) panel study. Donald Green provided me with the essential insight that a panel study could be created retrospectively. Ole Holsti and James Rosenau generously allowed me access to their 1988 Foreign Policy Leadership Project (FPLP) sample list and questionnaires and gave me valuable advice. David Kinsella supplied the codes that permitted respondents to remain anonymous. The John D. and Catherine T. MacArthur Foundation and the Block Fund financed the project.

With regard to the separate task of interviewing people within the Bush administration, I owe thanks to Peter Hausloner. Without his help I would never have been able to get interviews with such high-level officials at the State Department, the National Security Council, and within the intelligence community. I also want to thank those officials for their time, but, by their wishes, they will remain anonymous.

The following people read either a portion of the manuscript or its entirety at one stage or another and offered valuable insights: Robert Abelson, Martin Gilens, Donald Green, Elizabeth Hanson, Thomas Hartley, Ole Holsti, William Kincade, David Mayhew, Rogers Smith, Allan Stam, and Valerie Sulfaro. I want to thank David Lumsdaine, in particular, for his detailed and insightful critique of an earlier draft. Also, Joanne Dionne helped me with data tape information, and Shannon Lauterbach and Jason Meyers assisted me with the preparation of the final manuscript.

My greatest debts are to Bruce Russett for his wise and careful guidance—this work is much better for his many contributions to it—and to Jonathan Cowden for his keen criticism and warm encouragement, and for tirelessly reading, editing, and improving drafts throughout the writing process.

CHAPTER 1

Introduction

For Americans, the end of the Cold War was not only a transformation of the international arena, it was the collapse of a paradigm. Containment had been the organizing principle of U.S. foreign policy for over four decades (Gaddis 1982). As Charles William Maynes (1990, 5), the editor of *Foreign Policy* magazine, eloquently observed, "American foreign policy will lose more than its enemy. It will lose the sextant by which the ship of state has been guided since 1945."

How deeply, then, have American leaders been affected by the Soviet collapse? Have they recast their most basic beliefs about the role the United States should play in the world? Or have they made more limited attitudinal adjustments in response to this profound environmental change? Knowledge about the depth of leaders' reactions will give us an important clue about the sources of their foreign policy beliefs: about the extent to which those beliefs reflect external circumstances or events or, conversely, about the extent to which they are an expression of more general values or ideological stances that apply to the domestic arena as well. The central purpose of this book is to investigate how much American leaders' foreign policy opinions changed once they revised their views about the Soviet Union, and to explore what that finding tells us about the sources and structure of their belief systems.

Past research has focused, by and large, on people's interpretations of circumstances within the international environment on the assumption that these interpretations are the primary source for their foreign policy beliefs. The realist tradition presupposes that it is not statesmen's "motives and . . . ideological preferences" that guide a nation's foreign policy, but rather their recognition of objective national interests within a given context (Morgenthau [1948] 1993, 5). Cognitive theories as well have focused on people's reactions to major events, especially wars, as the source of later beliefs (Roskin 1974; Holsti and Rosenau 1984)[1] or on individuals' perceptions about a foreign adversary as the key variable structuring other opinions (Cottam 1977; Herrmann 1986; Hurwitz and Peffley 1990; Koopman, Snyder, and Jervis 1990; Peffley and Hurwitz 1992). Finally, most accounts of the broad organizing dimensions thought to underlie Americans' foreign policy attitudes use descriptive terms relevant only to international politics and not applicable to domestic issues (Bardes and Oldendick 1978; Wittkopf 1981, 1990; Chittick and Billingsley 1989; Holsti and Rosenau 1990, 1993; Hinckley 1988).

The end of the Cold War offers a rare opportunity to explore the causal connection between external circumstances and Americans' belief systems. While it is true that, for Americans, the denouement of the Cold War was a peaceful process and therefore perhaps less shocking and traumatic than some past wars, the event still marked an enormous change within the international environment. George Will (1989, 90), a political commentator, described 1989—the year the Berlin Wall came down—as the "most startling, interesting, promising and consequential year *ever*." Holsti and Rosenau (1993, 236) observe,

> One can make a reasonable argument that, taken together, the monumental events of the past half decade—including but not limited to the disintegration of the USSR, [and the] vast political change in Eastern Europe . . . —represent international changes of a magnitude that could be expected to effect fundamental changes in ways of thinking about international affairs.

Further, if Americans' perceptions about the former Soviet Union did in fact dictate many other foreign policy beliefs—as posited by some past research—then we could expect deep attitudinal change to accompany the end of the Cold War.

Using panel survey data, this study tests the proposition that the Soviet collapse was a watershed event that caused a wholesale change in American leaders' foreign policy beliefs. Most of the evidence used here is drawn from the Leadership Opinion Project (LOP) panel study. A panel study, by definition, is a research design in which data are collected at two or more points in time for the same individuals or cases. In this instance, 660 opinion leaders (people selected from *Who's Who*, State Department officials, media leaders, foreign policy experts outside government, politicians, and clergy) answered questionnaires both before and after the series of events that cumulatively ended the Cold War. The first wave of the LOP panel study was administered in 1988, more than a year before the demolition of the Berlin Wall; the second wave was administered in 1992, months after the Soviet Union had collapsed. As a result, this unique data set provides a before-and-after snapshot of the attitudes held by elite political actors in the United States. (For a detailed discussion of the way the LOP panel study was constructed, see appendix A.)

I will show that the upheavals in the international arena had only limited ramifications on the foreign policy beliefs of American leaders. Not surprisingly, the LOP respondents recognized that the Soviet military threat and the ideological challenge of communism had dissipated, and most adjusted their attitudes on related policies. Their opinions about defense spending, for example, or about the stationing of troops in Europe, changed in accordance with the new realities. But, at the same time, some of the respondents' most basic orientations toward international affairs, such as their attitudes about the use of military force, remained quite stable.

To be sure, even the simple recognition that the world is a less threatening place will have a profound impact on American foreign policy. Without their longtime adversary, American leaders will be free to address new strategic and domestic issues. My findings suggest, however, that opinion leaders have adhered to their old postures about how the United States should conduct itself in the world.

By the end of the 1980s, there were signs of a consensus among scholars that two primary factors or dimensions were necessary, if not sufficient, to characterize the beliefs of American elites and the mass public in the post-Vietnam era (Wittkopf 1990; Holsti and Rosenau 1990; for a different view, see Chittick and Billingsley 1989). One dimension, labeled *militant internationalism,* involved people's attitudes about the use of force abroad and the related issue of containment. The second dimension, labeled *cooperative internationalism,* denoted people's attitudes about efforts to solve common problems or to help other countries. Put another way, these two dimensions constituted some of the most basic orientations of Americans concerning *how* the United States should deal with other countries. By tracking respondents' placement on these dimensions over time, I will show that their general postures were not buffeted by the dramatic events surrounding the end of the Cold War.

How can we explain this surprising continuity in leaders' foreign policy beliefs despite the end of the Cold War? A plausible explanation is close at hand: if leaders' basic beliefs about how the United States should interact with other countries were derived from the same source as their domestic preferences, say, common core values, then we would expect belief stability even within the context of profound international change.

The notion of a linkage between the foreign policy and domestic domains—at least for elites—is scarcely novel or farfetched. It is true that Converse, during the 1950s, found a "falling off of constraint *between* the domains of domestic and foreign policy, relative to the high level of constraint *within* each domain" and explained it as signifying "boundaries between belief systems that are relatively independent" (1964, 229; emphasis in original). However, scholars later reported evidence that led to the opposite conclusion. Russett and Hanson (1975), in a study of business and military leaders, found that respondents' positions on domestic issues were a powerful predictor of their foreign policy attitudes; these authors surmised that the Vietnam War had served as a catalyst to bring foreign policy views in line with domestic policy preferences (1975, 130–44; see also Hughes 1978).[2] And numerous studies about congressional representatives—yet another leadership group— also revealed an alignment on foreign policy issues according to ideological orientations (e.g., Russett 1970; Moyer 1973; Bernstein and Anthony 1974; Fleisher 1985; Sulfaro 1995). Schneider, for instance, argued that "a *single dimension*—perhaps recognizable as the left-right dimension characteristic of European politics—structures congressional voting and foreign policy attitudes in the period 1971–76" (1979, 147; emphasis in original). More recently, Holsti and Rosenau (1988, 277), using 1984 survey data, found that American opinion leaders' "responses to many domestic and foreign policy issues follow a consistent pattern of overlapping cleavages that finds liberals on one side and conservatives on the other." When Holsti (1994, 26) updated this analysis using 1992 data, he concluded that "the strong relationship between domestic and foreign policy beliefs uncovered in responses to the 1984 leadership survey has persisted through the early post–Cold War years." Judging from these various empirical studies, then, it is certainly conceivable that leaders' basic foreign policy postures were derived from the same source as their domestic beliefs.

Using the LOP panel data, I will explore the dynamic relationships between different beliefs over a period of time that incorporates the end of the Cold War. The argument I employ here owes much to a theory about belief structures usually associated with Philip Converse.[3] Converse (1964, 207) defines a belief system as "a configuration of ideas and attitudes in which the elements are bound together by some form of constraint or functional interdependence." He observes that *constraint* can be either static or dynamic. "In the static case," he argues that

> "constraint" may be taken to mean the success we would have in predicting, given initial knowledge that an individual holds a specified attitude, that he holds certain further ideas and attitudes. (1964, 207)

"In the dynamic case," Converse continues,

"constraint" or "interdependence" refers to the probability that a change in the perceived status (truth, desirability, and so forth) of one idea-element would *psychologically* require, from the point of view of the actor, some compensating change(s) in the status of idea-elements elsewhere in the configuration. (1964, 208; emphasis in original)

A researcher can use cross-sectional data to locate static constraint between attitudes, but only panel data will reveal dynamic constraint. (See appendix B for a general discussion about the differences between panel data and cross-sectional data.)

Some scholars posited that Americans' stereotypes about the former Soviet Union had served to constrain both specific policy stances, such as defense spending, and more general postures, such as militarism (Hurwitz and Peffley 1990; Peffley and Hurwitz 1992; see also Herrmann 1986; Koopman, Snyder, and Jervis 1990). The end of the Cold War allows us to disentangle the interrelationships between these different attitudes for the first time. We can look for evidence of dynamic constraint in leaders' belief systems: that is, we can observe whether changes in respondents' evaluations about Russia over time are accompanied by changes in other beliefs as well.

I will demonstrate that dynamic constraint did not exist between leaders' images of the Soviet Union and their basic foreign policy postures. Respondents' images about Russia changed between the two waves of the LOP panel study, but their more general orientations toward international affairs remained stable. This finding suggests little "functional interdependence" between these "idea-elements," to use Converse's terms. If opinion leaders possessed schemas about the Soviet Union that organized other beliefs, then these mental constructs had a narrow scope limited only to certain security policies.[4]

At first glance, this research finding may appear counterintuitive. After all, we know that U.S. leaders were preoccupied with policies aimed at containing Soviet influence for decades; we know that managing relations with the Soviet Union was the most important foreign policy challenge the United States faced after the Second World War. How, then, can we doubt the importance of this issue within elite belief systems?

A distinction must be made between issues that are priorities within public policy and attitudes that play a central causal role within individuals' belief systems. The term *centrality,* when applied to belief systems, has a particular meaning. Central beliefs are more resistant to change than peripheral beliefs, but once they change, the ramifications for the belief system are large (Converse 1964, 208; Rokeach [1968] 1972, 23). And while it is true that policies about how to deal with the Soviet Union dominated the U.S. foreign policy agenda, leaders' beliefs about their main adversary appear not to have been highly central. American leaders' perceptions about the nature and motives of the Soviet Union changed without sending far-reaching reverberations throughout their belief systems: some basic postures, namely, stances toward cooperative internationalism and militant internationalism were hardly touched. In other words, leaders' images of the Soviet Union were not causally prior to these general postures.[5]

Constraint over time is evident, however, between respondents' foreign policy postures and their domestic policy preferences: these idea-elements are substantially associated with each other both in 1988 and 1992, and all remained quite stable across the two waves of the LOP study. This evidence is consistent with the interpretation that leaders' domestic ideological orientations and core values—variables that did not change en masse with the disintegration of the Soviet Union— anchored and restrained their foreign policy postures as the Cold War ended. Such evidence on the absence of change might be likened to the Sherlock Holmes clue of the "dog who didn't bark."

One assumption implied in Converse's (1964) original theory, in more recent analyses of panel data (e.g., Peffley and Hurwitz 1992), and in my own research, concerns the nature of causality in belief systems. The terms *constraint* and *functional interdependence* imply a causal relationship between attitudes. The term *dynamic constraint* involves little more than simple causal logic: if x causes y, then a change in x will produce a change in y. The variables involved, however, are separate, identifiable idea-elements within a larger belief system. Following this logic, I essentially argue that

(a) American opinion leaders' mental images of the Soviet Union changed dramatically between 1988 and 1992; but,

(b) some of their basic foreign policy postures (militant internationalism and cooperative internationalism) remained stable over the same time period; which shows that,

(c) leaders' perceptions about the Soviet Union were not an important source of constraint for these foreign policy postures. Yet,

(d) another variable—namely, respondents' domestic ideological orientations—is substantially associated with their foreign policy postures in both years, and across time; and,

(e) this other variable also remained stable between the two waves of the panel study; therefore,

(f)   opinion leaders' domestic ideological orientations constrained their foreign policy postures and anchored respondents' reactions to the end of the Cold War. Finally,

(g)   as respondents' basic foreign policy postures and their ideological orientations both remained stable over time, the gap dividing opinion leaders on foreign policy issues has not lessened much with the end of the Cold War.

It is possible that the mechanisms that operate within belief systems are much more complicated.[6] However, the theoretical assumption that the connections between idea-elements within elite belief systems are subject to simple causal processes allows us to push this investigation as far as the LOP panel data permit.

What, then, is the nature of the linkage between leaders' domestic beliefs and their foreign policy beliefs? A few scholars have pointed to core values as the source of both domestic and foreign policy beliefs (Rokeach 1973; Lumsdaine 1993).[7] In this view, there is not a clear demarcation between values relevant to domestic situations and values relevant to foreign policy. As Lumsdaine (1993, 22) observes, the "beliefs, values, and practices of daily moral discourse and domestic political life tend to be transferred to one's understanding and conduct of foreign affairs."

Other research suggests that separate values are not free-floating: certain values appear to "go together" and, as a result, may be arrayed along an ideological continuum (McClosky 1958; McClosky and Zaller 1984, chap. 7).[8] Zaller concisely describes the connection between values and political ideology as follows:

> many people . . . respond to different value dimensions *as if* they were organized by a common left-right dimension. There is, in other words, a tendency for people to be fairly consistently "left" or "right" or "centrist" on such disparate value dimensions as economic individualism, opinions toward communists, tolerance of nonconformists, racial issues, sexual freedom, and religious authority. (1992, 26; emphasis in original)

Unfortunately, however, the values literature, at least in political science, is sparse.

Combining these insights, I argue that elite political actors apply the same or kindred values to circumstances at home and abroad. These values—and the corresponding attitudes about policy—are loosely tied together into "cognitive packages" to which the labels *conservatism* and *liberalism* may be attached. For American leaders, these labels possess meaning whether applied to the domestic or the foreign policy domain.

Using this framework, respondents' reaction to the end of the Cold War makes sense. Americans now face circumstances that would have been unthinkable during the Cold War. But while the international arena has been transformed, the basic values that inform individuals' foreign policy stances, and that divide liberals from conservatives, have remained constant. And because leaders draw upon long-held values to evaluate new international circumstances, their beliefs about the proper way to conduct foreign policy were largely unchanged.

An important side issue, regarding the dimensionality of elite beliefs, is raised by this explanation. As I noted earlier, by the late 1980s, there were signs of an emerging consensus among scholars that Wittkopf's militant internationalism (MI)/cooperative internationalism (CI) scheme accurately characterized the foreign policy beliefs of both American elites and the mass public (Wittkopf 1990; Holsti and Rosenau 1990). Researchers identified four belief types by using people's placements along these two orthogonal dimensions:[9] hard-liners (support MI, oppose CI), accommodationists (oppose MI, support CI), internationalists (support MI, support CI), and isolationists (oppose MI, oppose CI).

This more nuanced categorization of Americans' foreign policy beliefs seemed to better capture the post-Vietnam disagreements than the conventional left-to-right continuum. But, at the same time, there is substantial empirical verification (as noted earlier) that elites' foreign policy beliefs are closely associated with their domestic beliefs: that a left-to-right dimension does structure elites' attitudes across both policy domains.

How, then, can we square the description of Americans' foreign policy beliefs as bidimensional with other research that highlights, at least within leaders' belief systems, the importance of a single liberalism/ conservatism dimension? Are the dimensions that organize leaders' foreign policy beliefs different than the dimensions that organize their domestic beliefs? These are some additional questions that I will address in this book.[10]

The book is organized as follows. Chapter 2 provides the political backdrop for the LOP panel study. The chapter relies both on historical data (e.g., personal interviews with government officials, public statements of national security elites, and journalistic accounts) and elite survey data (both trend and panel data). Together, this evidence illustrates that American opinion leaders were still suspicious of the Soviet Union in the spring of 1988—when the first panel wave was administered. The events that marked the end of the Cold War—the revolutions in Eastern Europe—occurred more than a year later. And, by 1992, when the second panel wave was administered, American opinion leaders' perceptions about Russia and containment had already been transformed. Put simply, the chapter shows that the two waves of the LOP panel study bracket the end of the Cold War.

In chapter 3, I demonstrate that leaders' basic foreign policy orientations (defined as militant and cooperative internationalism) were not buffeted by the end of the Cold War. The first portion of this chapter reviews past research findings about the broad organizing dimensions or factors that underlie Americans' foreign policy beliefs, as well as theories about how people's images of the Soviet Union structured their other beliefs. I then measure respondents' basic postures regarding the use of military force and involvement in cooperative ventures abroad, and show that their positions on these scales remained quite stable over time. Because respondents' attitudes toward Russia and containment policy changed between the waves of the panel study and their basic postures remained stable, we can infer that dynamic constraint between these idea-elements did not exist.

Chapter 4 addresses the question of why leaders' postures remained stable. First, I demonstrate the association between respondents' ideological orientations and their foreign policy postures over time. Second, I develop an explanation consistent with this empirical finding: I argue that the philosophies of conservatism and liberalism tie together values that apply to issues both within and beyond the domestic borders, and that these underlying values have remained constant. Third, as this explanation raises a question about the dimensionality of elite beliefs, I demonstrate that the liberal-to-conservative continuum does indeed have much relevance within the foreign policy as well as the domestic domain, even if it is not the *only* dimension underlying beliefs in either.

Chapter 5 discusses some political implications that may stem from the continuity found in opinion leaders' beliefs. Analysts who hope that the Soviet collapse will allow the emergence of bipartisan politics may be disappointed. I show that important divisions between ideological groups have outlived the Cold War. Indeed, American leaders appear to have interpreted lessons from the end of the Cold War in a manner consistent with their past postures and ideological stances. I also argue that continued divisiveness among ideological groups is consistent with the explanation found in chapter 4: that is, leaders who embrace different values and political philosophies have disagreed about foreign policy issues in the past, and because their basic values remained constant despite transformations in the international arena, they will continue to disagree in the future.

Chapter 6 is a brief conclusion. It summarizes what we have learned about leaders' reactions to recent major events in the international arena. In particular, it highlights the dynamic between the "intellectual baggage" that people carry around with themselves and the process by which they interpret dramatically changed "objective" circumstances.[11] The LOP respondents acknowledged changes within the international arena and adjusted their beliefs accordingly, but they also adhered to old postures about how the United States should conduct itself in the world. Most important, leaders' core values and ideological orientations served as "anchors against change" once the Cold War ended.

CHAPTER 2

When Did the Cold War End?

Can we demarcate a point in time when most American opinion leaders came to believe the Cold War was over?[1] An implicit assumption underlying the inferences I make in later chapters concerns the timing of the Leadership Opinion Project (LOP) panel study in relation to the end of the Cold War. It is essential that the first wave of the panel was administered before this historical turning point and that the second was administered well after it had passed. Also, it is essential that the LOP respondents had enough time to recognize the momentous changes in the international arena and to adjust their beliefs. If these conditions were met, we would expect to find that respondents' attitudes about Russia and containment policy had been transformed between the two waves of the panel study. It is important to show that these attitudes in fact have changed before we consider the ramifications of the Soviet collapse on other foreign policy beliefs.

In this chapter, I will place the timing of the LOP panel study within a broader political context and thereby demonstrate that the Cold War, as perceived by most American leaders, ended in the interim between waves. The discussion begins with a brief characterization of the different images that American leaders had of the Soviet Union in the past. I will then pinpoint when Americans' beliefs about the Soviet threat changed in reaction to international events. Finally, I will demonstrate that, as expected, a sea change in respondents' attitudes toward Russia and containment policy did occur within the time span of the LOP study.

Past Perceptions about the Soviet Union

American opinion leaders had perceived the Soviet Union as their principal adversary since the Second World War. Animosity toward the Soviets was derived as much from ideological as from geopolitical considerations: anticommunism runs deep within American culture (Caute 1978). In short, there was a consensus within the United States that the Soviet leadership had political objectives antithetical to American values and interests.

11

Within this broader consensus, however, American leaders embraced different stereotypes about their enemy. Scholars have provided numerous typologies that categorize the positions of policymakers and foreign policy experts into defined groups or belief clusters. Although some scholars made additional, more nuanced distinctions (e.g., Dallin and Lapidus 1983; Herrmann 1985), all incorporated a hard-line and a soft-line perspective (e.g., Sanders 1983b; Yergin 1977; see also Jervis 1976; Snyder and Diesing 1977). A basic cleavage existed, particularly after the Vietnam War, between those American opinion leaders who believed that U.S. military superiority and vigilant containment of the Soviet Union provided the best means of securing peace, and those who emphasized more accommodating tactics by the United States such as the pursuit of arms control (Tetlock 1983).[2]

Survey data from the 1970s and 1980s have corroborated the existence of this schism. The differences among American opinion leaders were apparent, for instance, in Holsti and Rosenau's (1984, 1986) identification of three belief clusters in their 1976, 1980, and 1984 Foreign Policy Leadership Project (FPLP) samples. Two of these belief clusters—"Cold War Internationalists" and "Post–Cold War Internationalists"[3]—incorporated hard-line and soft-line perspectives, respectively, on the Soviet Union .[4] The "Cold War Internationalists" were

> inclined to view the international system as bipolar in structure. A relentless Soviet drive against the United States and its allies, buttressed by a rapid military buildup in the USSR, is thus the primary threat. . . . Moscow's determination to expand its influence by whatever means is the unvarying driving force behind Kremlin policies. In order to forestall the threat, it is vital for the United States and the West to maintain a high level of military capabilities, a determination to match or exceed increases in Soviet force levels and a willingness to use military power if necessary to discourage adventures by the USSR. (Holsti and Rosenau 1986, 379)

In contrast, "Post–Cold War Internationalists" tended

> to view the international system and primary threats to its stability in terms of North-South issues, including but not limited to the growing gap between rich and poor nations, threats to the environment, population, resources, racial conflict, trade, Third World debts, and other international economic issues. . . . Détente, arms control, and other such measures can not only stabilize relations between the superpowers but they also permit some of the re-

sources that have, for example, gone into arms races to be used for dealing with the longer-range threats to mankind. (Holsti and Rosenau 1986, 379)

In other words, respondents were distinguished, in part, by how much emphasis they placed on the "Soviet threat" as the source of international problems, and by the types of tactics they advocated for dealing with that country.

At the core of opinion leaders' differences lay divergent perceptions about the nature of their adversary: they disagreed about whether the Soviet Union was so abhorrent and aggressive that the only means available to modify its behavior involved the use of force. Hard-liners embraced an image of the Soviet Union as articulated in National Security Council report NSC-68:

the Soviet Union, unlike previous aspirants to hegemony, is animated by a new fanatic faith, antithetical to our own, and seeks to impose its absolute authority over the rest of the world. Conflict has, therefore, become endemic and is waged, on the part of the Soviet Union, by violent or non-violent methods in accordance with the dictates of expediency. (National Security Council [1950] 1993, 25)

The Russians, in this view, were different than other people: the tactics of compromise and accommodation would not work; they understood "only force" (Barnet 1981, 45). Tetlock (1983, 70) characterizes the core policy assumption of this viewpoint as follows: "One increases the likelihood of war by trying to appease aggressors. To avoid disaster, status quo powers must clearly communicate their willingness to go to war."

In contrast, adherents of the soft-line perspective emphasized the similarities between Russians and Americans. They observed that both countries were susceptible to misperceptions about the other, and that these misperceptions, in turn, fed the arms race. The Soviet leadership, they pointed out, shared the same human reactions to threats and conflict situations as Americans did. As Tetlock (1983, 71–72) notes, adherents of this view believed that confrontational tactics only intensify a dangerous situation: indeed, "mutual fear often destabilizes rather than stabilizes the international system." The way to tame our adversary, then, was to seek out issue areas of mutual interest such as arms control.

Consequently, political elites within the United States struggled with each other over the appropriate policy toward the Soviet Union, especially during the 1970s and 1980s.[5] When Jimmy Carter took office in 1976, he expressed a view, shared by many of his colleagues at the recently founded Trilateral Commission, that East-West relations could now be downgraded (Sanders 1983b; Barnet 1981). The United States, he told the rest of the country, now confronted many important world problems that had nothing to do with the aspirations of the Soviet Union, problems such as the scarcity of natural resources, economic relations among industrialized countries, and conflicts between the northern and southern hemispheres. In his Notre Dame commencement address on May 22, 1977, Carter proclaimed that the "threat of conflict with the Soviet Union has become less intensive" (Carter 1977, 775). "For too many years," he argued,

> we've been willing to adopt the flawed and erroneous principles and tactics of our adversaries, sometimes abandoning our own values for theirs. We've fought fire with fire, never thinking that fire is better quenched with water. (Carter 1977, 774)

Now, Carter declared, we have freed ourselves "of that inordinate fear of communism that once led us to embrace any dictator who joined us in that fear" (Carter 1977, 774). Most important, Carter attempted to continue the policy of détente during his administration in the form of the SALT II Treaty.

President Carter's efforts, however, were attacked by influential critics on the right. Opposition to the policy of détente had mobilized even before Carter was elected. The Coalition for a Democratic Majority, and, especially, the Committee on the Present Danger (CPD), brought together many high-profile leaders—public officials, foreign policy experts, journalists, academics, and corporate executives (Sanders 1983a, 154–60).[6] Together, these organizations (along with others, such as the American Security Council) sent a loud message to opposing elites and to the mass public: the Soviet threat was still a clear and present danger.[7]

The fundamental flaw of détente policy, according to conservative critics, was that it ignored the fact that Soviet intentions to dominate the world had remained unchanged; it thereby robbed the West of the will to fight back. Eugene Rostow, a former undersecretary of state during the Johnson administration, head of the Coalition for a Democratic Majority, and then a founding member of the CPD, articulated this view in 1976:

> The situation in the world recalls that of the Thirties. The pressure of Soviet policy is increasing steadily, but the perception of the threat in the West has been diminishing. This strange psychological

phenomenon is the heart of our foreign policy problem today. (Sanders 1983a, 162)

Prominent critics from these organizations charged the Nixon, Ford, and Carter administrations with allowing the Soviet Union to surpass the United States in military power. In response to their sustained pressure, Gerald Ford dropped the term *détente* before the 1976 presidential campaign, and Carter also moderated his prodétente policies (Sanders 1983a). In one of their most effective mobilizations, these groups targeted the SALT II Treaty that Carter had signed with Leonid Brezhnev, the general secretary of the Soviet Union, in 1979.[8]

The Soviet invasion of Afghanistan reinforced an already apparent swing to the right among elite political actors in the United States (Ferguson 1986; Ferguson and Rogers 1986).[9] President Carter, in particular, altered his expressed beliefs about the Soviet Union. He proclaimed in his 1980 State of the Union address that the invasion "could pose the most serious threat to world peace since the second World War" (Carter 1980, 227). He had come into office with promises "to create a wider framework of international cooperation" (Carter 1977, 778). But by the end of his term, Carter had changed his tune: he presented a defense budget with a substantial spending increase, withdrew the doomed SALT II Treaty from consideration in the Senate, and articulated what became known as the "Carter doctrine"—a promise that the United States would use force to protect its interests in the Persian Gulf. But it was the election of Ronald Reagan to the presidency that allowed the CPD's hard-line political views to again become national policy.[10]

During most of his first term, Reagan relentlessly preached about the Soviet threat and avidly sought U.S. military superiority. He presided over the largest peacetime military buildup in U.S. history (Lemann 1984).[11] The Reagan doctrine proclaimed a U.S. commitment to assist insurgencies against Moscow-supported regimes or, in other words, a commitment to "roll back" Soviet influence in places such as Nicaragua and Afghanistan. Further, the Reagan administration—striving to build up the U.S. nuclear arsenal and distrusting the Soviet Union's word in negotiations—eschewed many arms control negotiations (Garthoff 1994; Huntington 1983). Many political observers charged that, in order to pacify public opinion in the United States and Western Europe, American officials proposed baldly one-sided proposals, such as the "Zero Option" or START, with the advance knowledge that the Soviets could only reject them (Talbott 1984).[12]

When Gorbachev ascended to power in March 1985, the lines of debate between different political camps within the United States had long been drawn. American opinion leaders had embraced different images about the nature of the Soviet Union and consequently disagreed about policy. As many scholars have pointed out, such images, once formed, are quite resistant to change (e.g., Holsti 1967; Jervis 1976; Tetlock 1983; Silverstein and Flamenbaum 1989; Silverstein and Holt 1989; Koopman, Snyder, and Jervis 1989, 1990).[13] Therefore, nobody foresaw that the decades-old American debate about the appropriate policy toward the Soviet Union would soon be overhauled. After all, what could possibly happen to budge American elites' hardened images about the Soviet leadership?

Gorbachev's First Moves, 1985 to mid-1988

In May 1988, Georgi Arbatov, then director of the U.S.A. Institute and an advisor to Mikhail Gorbachev, made an unusual "threat" to the United States.[14] "We are going to do something terrible to you," he said. "We are going to take away your enemy" (Blumenthal 1990, 5). The Soviet leadership eventually succeeded in doing just that. As Raymond Garthoff (1992, 129) has succinctly argued, Gorbachev "brought the Cold War to an end" by renouncing "the idea of inevitable world conflict":

> His avowed acceptance of the interdependence of the world, of the priority of all-human values over class values, and of the indivisibility of common security marked a revolutionary ideological change. That change, which Gorbachev declared as early as 1986 (though insufficiently noted), manifested itself in many ways over the next five years, in deeds as well as in words, including policies reflecting a drastically reduced Soviet perception of the Western threat and actions to reduce the Western perception of the Soviet threat.[15]

Gorbachev's reconceptualization of Soviet foreign policy goals— away from the advancement of communism and toward a notion of common security—was first publicly evident in his Political Report to the Twenty-seventh Party Congress of the Soviet Communist Party held in early 1986 (Oberdorfer 1991, 159–60).[16] Gorbachev listed "principled considerations" that he said had guided policy under his leadership (Oberdorfer 1991, 159). These considerations reflected new thinking about security in the nuclear age:

> Because of "the character of contemporary weapons," Gorbachev argued, no state can defend itself through "military-technical means

alone" even with "the most powerful defense." The insurance of security "increasingly is a political task, and can be resolved only by political means" (Garthoff 1994, 259).

About the U.S.-Soviet relationship, Gorbachev said that "security . . . can only be mutual. . . . The highest wisdom is not in worrying only about oneself, or, all the more, about damaging the other side; it is necessary for all to feel that they are equally secure" (Oberdorfer 1991, 160).

Gorbachev stated that the modern "world has become too small and fragile for wars and policies of force. . . . This means realizing that it is in fact impossible to win the arms race, just as it is impossible to win a nuclear war itself. . . . Therefore it is essential above all to considerably reduce the level of military confrontation" (Oberdorfer 1991, 160).

In the "present situation," Gorbachev continued, "there is no alternative to cooperation and interaction between all states. Thus objective, and I stress objective, conditions have arisen in which the confrontation between capitalism and socialism can take place only and exclusively in the forms of peaceful competition and peaceful rivalry" (Oberdorfer 1991, 160).

Gorbachev also spoke of "global problems affecting all humanity" that could only be resolved through "cooperation on a global scale" (Garthoff 1994, 257).

Gorbachev took some important initial steps that reflected this new perspective between 1985 and mid-1988 (the period before the first wave of the LOP panel was administered). For instance, in July 1985, Gorbachev announced a unilateral Soviet moratorium on nuclear testing, which took effect that August. He later extended its deadline three times—for eighteen months—before allowing the moratorium to expire in February 1987 (Hertsgaard 1988, 289). In January 1986, he proposed a plan for the elimination all nuclear weapons by the year 2000: a plan that included major concessions by the Soviets during the first phase, but with the condition that the "development, testing and deployment" of the Strategic Defense Initiative (SDI) be stopped (Oberdorfer 1991, 156–57; Garthoff 1994, 252–53).

Similarly, at the summit in Reykjavik in October 1986, Gorbachev sprang a surprise proposal to reduce sharply the nuclear arsenals of both countries. Again, he made major concessions on the Soviet side.

He proposed a 50 percent cut in all major categories of strategic nuclear weapons (ICBMs, SLBMs, and heavy bombers), and, as *Washington Post* reporter and author Don Oberdorfer (1991, 191) notes, "for the first time" the Soviets "accepted major cuts in the big Soviet heavy missiles, for which there was no U.S. counterpart"—a concession that "had long been one of the most important U.S. objectives." Regarding intermediate-range missiles in Europe, Gorbachev proposed that the United States and the Soviet Union eliminate all their weapons, without requiring the British or French to scrap their intermediate-range nuclear forces (INF) or even to freeze them at existing levels (Garthoff 1994, 287). Oberdorfer (1991, 156–57, see also 191) notes that this INF proposal went a "long way toward accepting Reagan's 1981 'zero option' proposal . . . a proposal that had been ridiculed by many in the West as well as the East as one-sided and unnegotiable." However, Gorbachev added a proviso: research on SDI must be limited to the laboratory.[17]

Although this final point ultimately prevented an agreement, the magnitude of the changes that Reagan and Gorbachev discussed was unprecedented. In the heat of negotiations, the U.S. officials offered a counterproposal—called the Zero Ballistic Missiles proposal—to eliminate all ballistic missiles within ten years,[18] and remarkably, at one point, both countries appear to have endorsed the radical idea of eliminating nuclear weapons altogether (Shultz 1993, 772).

A few months later, in February 1987, Gorbachev announced another concession, permitting the negotiation of the INF Treaty. He agreed that this particular arms control proposal could be negotiated separately—that is, removed from their earlier stipulation, made at the Iceland meeting, that SDI research be limited (Garthoff 1994, 305). Reagan and Gorbachev signed the INF Treaty—the first agreement to eliminate a class of nuclear weapons—in Washington on December 8, 1987. It required the destruction, within three years, of 1,846 nuclear weapons on the Soviet side and 846 on the American side under strict inspection procedures (Oberdorfer 1991, 262).

Another important initiative proposed by the Soviet Union during Gorbachev's first three years concerned its withdrawal from Afghanistan. In September 1987, Eduard Shevardnadze, the Soviet foreign minister, first told Secretary of State George Shultz, privately, about the Soviets' intention to completely withdraw from Afghanistan before the end of Reagan's second term (Oberdorfer 1991, 234–35). The first public declaration of a timetable was reported on *Vremya*, a Soviet news program, on February 8, 1988: the announcer stated that Gorbachev had set a date to begin withdrawal—May 15—and the process was to be complete by March 15, 1989. The withdrawal was actually completed exactly one month earlier.

By mid-1988, Gorbachev had made some bold moves, especially in the realm of arms control, to reduce tensions with the United States and to challenge old perceptions of the Soviet Union. It is especially noteworthy that Gorbachev had begun to accept arms control proposals that blatantly favored the United States. Similar proposals had been offered by Reagan officials, many suspected, with the understanding that the terms were so one-sided as to be nonnegotiable. By accepting lopsided terms, Gorbachev was able to improve considerably the relations between the superpowers. As Gorbachev assessed the situation at the Washington summit in December 1987:

> I believe that what we have accomplished during the meeting and discussion will, with time, help considerably to improve the atmosphere in the world at large, and in America itself, in terms of its more correct and tolerant perception of my country, the Soviet Union.
>
> Today, the Soviet Union and the United States are closer to the common goals of strengthening international security. But this goal is yet to be reached. There is still much work to be done, and we must get down to it without delay. (Oberdorfer 1991, 271)

The Early Reaction of American Opinion Leaders

Opinion leaders within the United States responded to signs of change in their adversary with a mixture of optimism and wariness. Between 1985 and mid-1988, Americans began to question their perceptions about the Soviet Union, but the evidence was not yet convincing enough to vanquish old stereotypes.

The American establishment's reaction to the Reykjavik summit shows, first, the radical nature of the arms control proposals discussed there; and, second, that, for many, deep-seated suspicions about the Soviet Union's intentions remained largely unchanged by late 1986. National security elites were nothing less than appalled. There was some confusion as to whether the two countries had agreed at one point to the elimination of ballistic weapons in particular or to the elimination of all nuclear weapons.[19] But, regardless, news of the Iceland negotiations was received in Washington with a mixture of disbelief (that such proposals had been discussed) and relief (that SDI had blocked an agreement).

Criticism of the Iceland negotiations was bipartisan. Chairman Les Aspin, Democrat from Wisconsin, opened hearings in the House of

Representatives before the Defense Policy Panel of the Armed Services Committee with this statement:

> there is a very fundamental question out of Reykjavik about the way this administration handled the meeting. . . . [T]he concern is that we are dealing with fundamentally important issues, the security of our allies and ourselves, fundamental issues, and I think a lot of people were aghast and flabbergasted with the casual way things were tossed around. . . . I think Reykjavik itself has shaken a lot of people. (U.S. Congress 1986, 5)

Sam Nunn, Democrat from Georgia, went to the Senate floor and urged the president to "act immediately to pull our Zero Ballistic Missiles proposal off the table before the Soviets accept it" (Nunn 1986, 33164). He believed that the proposal would leave the United States in an inferior position to defend Western Europe.

Natural allies of the president also criticized the proposal. Admiral William Crowe, the chairman of the Joint Chiefs of Staff (JCS), told Reagan that the JCS had "concluded that the proposal to eliminate all ballistic missiles within 10 years time would pose high risks to the security of the nation" (Adelman 1989, 86). James Schlesinger, a former secretary of defense and a longtime critic of détente, argued in *Foreign Affairs* that

> Reykjavik had the potential for upsetting the military balance, for suddenly vitiating Western military strategy, and for destroying the cohesion of the Western alliance. . . . Reykjavik was a near disaster, and we should learn from it all that we can. Perhaps the best that can be said about the summit is that it was a *near* disaster. (1987, 437; emphasis in original; see also Schlesinger 1986)

At the heart of these critiques lay the perception that the Soviet threat had not fundamentally changed and that U.S. military strategy should not be impetuously altered. As Robert McNamara, former secretary of defense, observed during a congressional hearing:

> Is a nuclear-free world desirable? I believe it would be if it were attainable, and I think most Americans would agree. However, NATO's current military strategy and war plans are based on the opposite premise. And many—I would say most—U.S. military and civilian officials, as well as European leaders, hold the view that nuclear weapons are a necessary deterrent to Soviet aggression with

conventional forces. Therefore, they would not favor a world without nuclear weapons at this time. (U.S. Congress 1987a, 8–9)

American opinion leaders were not ready to discuss the removal of a single category of strategic weapons—ballistic missiles—much less the elimination of all nuclear weapons.

However, the INF Treaty—a treaty with much more limited aims— was greeted with approval. At the end of 1987, immediately following the Washington summit, *Time* magazine selected Gorbachev as "Man of the Year." The Senate resoundingly passed the INF Treaty during the summer of 1988, just days before Reagan left for the Moscow summit. This time, the skeptical James Schlesinger advised the Senate Committee on Foreign Relations to approve the treaty. In his prepared statement before the committee, Schlesinger discussed how the Soviets had to sacrifice many more weapons than the United States and called the treaty

> a remarkable achievement—quite astonishing in light of prior Soviet behavior in negotiations and probably quite implausible to those American officials who proposed the zero option in 1981. *At that time the proposal was viewed as so much in the American interest that the Soviets could never accept it.* Perhaps we might ponder this advice: never to look a gift horse in the mouth. But more appropriately, we should recognize that the Soviets have accepted a specific exchange lopsidedly in the Western interest for motives that, as yet, are not entirely clear to us. (U.S. Congress 1988a, 369– 70; emphasis added)

Still, a significant number of American opinion leaders did question Soviet motives. They could not believe the Soviets would agree to a treaty that favored American interests out of a sincere desire to reduce nuclear weapons or improve relations. Within the intelligence community, many thought that the "real thing" about the INF Treaty "was undermining NATO and destroying our strategic posture in Europe."[20] Skeptics believed that the Soviets' aim was to pour oil on the European peace movements; their ulterior motive was to denuclearize that region and to decouple American and European defense. As Professor William Van Cleave, a member of the original CPD executive committee and a well-known hawk,[21] testified before the Foreign Relations Committee:

> it seems . . . very likely that the Soviets' view of this [INF] agreement is that it will deeply undercut NATO strategy and very possibly

bring about the eventual denuclearization of U.S. forces in Europe. (U.S. Congress 1988a, 273–74)

Skeptics called Soviet reforms "cosmetic" and their new thinking "insincere." Senator Alfonse D'Amato, Republican of New York, articulated this perception:

> Has the Soviet bear become a lamb? Or is it merely trying on the fleece of civilized international behavior to win a temporary respite in its competition with the West? Once it has improved its relative position, will the Soviet Union simply return to its expansionist imperial policies? (U.S. Congress 1987b, 38)

Some American opinion leaders argued that the Soviet Union really wanted a breathing space to strengthen and revitalize itself. They pointed out that the Soviets were still communists. For instance, Henry Kissinger (1987, 34, 41), former secretary of state, wrote an article for *Newsweek* in which he deplored the mood of "euphoria sweeping Washington" during the 1987 summit and warned that Gorbachev "has never wavered from basic communist doctrine." Kissinger argued that Gorbachev was "in relentless pursuit of a strategic objective: to accelerate the loss of confidence in American strategic power, which throughout the postwar period has been the principal counterweight to Soviet conventional preponderance" (34). Richard Nixon (1989, 200, 204) later charged in a *Foreign Affairs* article that "reporters and diplomats alike have naively confused changes in style and rhetoric with shifts in substance and policy" and that "Gorbachev's public relations experts have made many Western policymakers forget that a more benign Soviet image does not mean a more benign Soviet foreign policy."

But the Reagan administration had not been swept away by Gorbachev's rhetoric (Garthoff 1994, 334–40). Secretary of State George Shultz (1988a, 7) commented in a December 1987 speech before the World Affairs Council that "There is nothing in the 'new political thinking' to date which suggests that the end of the adversarial struggle is at hand." He reiterated this theme in February 1988, stating that he found

> it difficult to believe that our relations with the Soviet Union will ever be "normal." . . . It seems unlikely that the U.S.-Soviet relationship will ever lose what always has been and is today a strongly wary and at times adversarial element. (Shultz 1988b, 41)

Likewise, President Reagan issued a policy paper entitled "National Security Strategy of the United States" in January 1988 that maintained a quite cautious tone. While we "hear talk of 'new thinking' and of basic changes in Soviet policies. . . . ," Reagan (1988, 1–2) wrote in the preface, "we have yet to see any slackening of the growth of Soviet military power, or abandonment of expansionist aspirations." The paper stated that "Despite some improvement in US-Soviet relations over the past year, the long-term threat has not perceptibly diminished. . . . [W]e must not delude ourselves into believing . . . that our vigilance can be reduced" (20).

Not surprisingly, the American right wing was contemptuous of the arms control efforts. Howard Phillips and Richard Viguerie called Reagan "nothing more than a useful idiot for Soviet propaganda" (Blumenthal 1990, 45). Other right-wingers used the term "Reagachev" to describe the president (Blumenthal 1990, 45). A full-page cartoon, signed by "many prominent conservatives, from Robert Bork to Norman Podhoretz," appeared in the *New York Times* on June 23, 1988, soon after the Moscow summit. "It depicted a glowering bear, with sharp fangs, clawing a helpless man in a business suit" (Blumenthal 1990, 249). The caption read, "Have We Forgotten That Every Time We've Hugged the Bear Somebody Else Has Suffered?":

> Now the bear is tired, wounded, and asking for our help. And our country is euphoric about giving it, forgetting that a wounded bear can be very dangerous. . . . [T]he United States can ill afford to assume that the bear has been tamed. (Blumenthal 1990, 249)

American opinion leaders did not react to the early signs of change in the Soviet Union with one voice. How, then, can we gauge the extent of change in leaders' opinions by mid-1988? I propose three rough measures. First, there is a singularly appropriate congressional report, dated September 1988, that expresses Democratic and Republican assessments of the changes in the Soviet military threat. Second, the 1988 presidential campaign reflects the public stances of both parties. Third, and most important, Holsti and Rosenau's 1988 FPLP survey provides data about opinion leaders' perceptions of the Soviet Union in the spring of that year. (Note that the LOP panel study was created by recontacting a portion of this sample. See appendix A.) All three indicators show that most American leaders were optimistic about the changes initiated by Gorbachev but still wary about how far these reforms would go and how long they would last. In other words, partisan leaders on both sides of the ideological spectrum were still tentative in their evaluations of the meaning, significance, and potential duration of changes within the Soviet Union. Few were ready to conclude that the Cold War was over by 1988.

Congressional Report on Changes in the Soviet Military

The first gauge of the changes in American leaders' beliefs by 1988 comes from a report by the Defense Policy Panel of the House Armed Services Committee entitled "General Secretary Mikhail Gorbachev and the Soviet Military: Assessing His Impact and the Potential for Future Changes." The panel's conclusions can be regarded as those of the Democratic members; almost all the Republican members signed a dissenting opinion.

The Democratic members of the panel believed that Gorbachev sincerely wanted to reform the Soviet military in order to redistribute scarce resources into the domestic sector. To do so, Gorbachev needed to redefine the Western threat and thereby change the rationale by which resources were allocated to the military. Arms control was a tool that Gorbachev had used to reach this goal. The real question, in the minds of these U.S. representatives, was whether Gorbachev had succeeded in convincing the Soviet military to change its doctrines and operations. The Democrats' conclusion was mixed. They found that, on the one hand, Gorbachev had not "caused any concrete, operational changes in Soviet military behavior." Yet, on the other hand, Gorbachev

> has changed the terms of debate. He has introduced a doctrinal justification for a reduced Soviet military establishment and actively pursued arms control initiatives intended to validate his new doctrine. The Soviet military, for its part, has been forced to justify its resource claims in the new language of "sufficiency" and "defense." (U.S. Congress 1988b, 12–13)

The panel believed that "[t]he INF Treaty and progress in START reflect an emerging consensus among Soviet political and military leaders on the implications of nuclear parity for Soviet security" (U.S. Congress 1988b, 19).

The Republican portion of the panel disagreed with this assessment. In their minds, the conclusion that Soviet nuclear doctrine had changed, and that the Soviets had abandoned goals of nuclear superiority or nuclear warfighting was wrong. "Soviet leaders," they argued, "have long used public statements announcing doctrinal 'changes' as a tool to influence Western public opinion" (U.S. Congress 1988b, 20). Consequently, they concluded,

Western leaders should continue to be exceedingly cautious in their approach to Gorbachev's "reform" initiatives, including promises of monumental arms control agreements. . . . We should wait for Soviet actions, not words, to demonstrate the degree to which they are serious about change. (U.S. Congress 1988b, 21)

In sum, neither the Democrats nor the Republicans were ready to declare the Cold War over. The Democratic assessment of Gorbachev's reforms was that they were genuine, that they had changed the doctrinal goals of the military, but that, on an operational level, they were still inchoate. As yet, it was impossible to tell the strength of Gorbachev's bargaining position vis-à-vis the Soviet military and hence how far reforms would go or how long they would endure. The Republicans went further. They disavowed the sincerity of Gorbachev. They held onto the belief that any doctrinal changes articulated by the Soviets were just words meant for Western consumption. In their view, the old goals of the Soviet leadership—from the spread of communism to nuclear superiority—had not changed.

The 1988 Presidential Campaign

The presidential campaign is another useful gauge for judging how far the public political debate had changed by 1988.[22] Like previous evidence, the party platforms also reveal that leaders on both sides of the political spectrum did not yet perceive the Cold War to be over. The Democrats again took the more optimistic position, stating that the Soviets' good will still had to be "tested":

We believe in an America that will promote peace and prevent war . . . not by relaxing our vigilance on the assumption that long-range Soviet interests have permanently changed . . . but . . . by testing the intentions of the new Soviet leaders. (Congressional Quarterly Almanac 1988a, 89A)

The Republican platform clung to the familiar Cold War tone: it proclaimed America's commitment to aid freedom fighters and resist "Marxist expansionism"; it stated that Republicans could best build on recent progress, "ever cautious of communism's long history of expansionism and false promises"; and it warned that

America cannot afford a future administration which eagerly attempts to embrace perceived, but as yet unproven, changes in Soviet

policy. Nor can we indulge naive inexperience or an overly enthusias-
tic endorsement of current Soviet rhetoric. (Congressional Quarterly
Almanac 1988b, 66A; see also Rosenbaum 1992)

The nominees themselves exuded a cautious optimism, at best,
about Soviet reforms (Blumenthal 1990). A Bush commercial epito-
mized the Republican campaign strategy. It showed Bush shaking
Gorbachev's hand in front of the White House. Reagan stood to one
side. The voice-over said "Somebody is going to find out if he's real.
This is no time for uncertainty. This is the time for strength" (Blumenthal 1990, 317). Robert Teeter, Bush's campaign pollster, had advised
the vice president that Americans' anxiety about the ability of the next
president to deal with Gorbachev would help him and that they should
play up the Soviet threat (Beschloss and Talbott 1993, 9).

Whether for tactical reasons or from conviction, Bush's campaign
rhetoric was decidedly cool with regard to Gorbachev.[23] In January 1988,
he remarked at the National Press Club that Gorbachev was not a
"freedom-loving friend of democracy" but an "orthodox, committed
Marxist" (Beschloss and Talbott 1993, 9). In a March address, billed as
his "vision speech," Bush said that "Clearly something is happening in
the Soviet Union. . . . In time we'll know if it's only cosmetic" (Blumenthal 1990, 107). In his first debate with Michael Dukakis, the Democratic nominee, Bush stated that "the jury is still out on the Soviet
experiment" (Beschloss and Talbott 1993, 10).

Dukakis was also cautious. In June 1988, he presented a major
foreign policy speech at the Atlantic Council. "According to his aides,"
reported Don Oberdorfer in the *Washington Post,*

Dukakis' main aim was to persuade the audience of foreign and
defense policy experts and U.S. allies that he is "not another
George McGovern" promising drastic changes in U.S. foreign policy as did the 1972 Democratic nominee. (Blumenthal 1990, 234)

After the speech, Joseph Nye, a Harvard professor and one of Dukakis's
foreign policy campaign advisors, flew to Paris to address a diplomatic
audience at the French Institute for International Relations. He reas-
sured the group that with Dukakis as president there would be "[n]o
more Reykjaviks" and "no free gift" for Gorbachev (Blumenthal 1990,
235).

On September 13, 1988, Dukakis told an audience at the Chicago
Council on Foreign Relations (CCFR) that he was the man best qualified for "testing the limits of what is called 'new thinking' in the Soviet

Union." He outlined positions for expanded cooperation with the Soviet Union in return for "improved Soviet behavior in world affairs." And his campaign strategists crafted a telling photo opportunity to accompany news reports about the speech: that day, Dukakis flew to the General Dynamics tank plant in Sterling Heights, Michigan, put on an army helmet and a flak suit, clutched a machine gun, and rode around in a tank (Reid 1988, A4).

After the election, Sidney Blumenthal (1990, 318), author and senior editor at the *New Republic,* asked Nye about the Dukakis campaign strategy regarding changes in East-West relations. Nye responded,

> The end of the Cold War? It came up. There was still some uncertainty of whether the Soviets were going to follow up good rhetoric with good proposals. To declare the Cold War over when there were no changes in Soviet force structure was a little bit early. Were people a little bit cautious? Yes. It was unclear. We struck a cautionary note. We were not there yet. It was almost conventional wisdom that a Democrat on defense issues had to be cautious and careful in order not to be painted into a position that George Bush eventually painted Dukakis.

Judging by the presidential campaign, American opinion leaders were open to the possibility that the Soviet reforms might bring a fundamental change in superpower relations. But, by 1988, even the optimists were only at the stage of saying "let's wait and see" whether the Soviet leadership's new rhetoric and behavior are real.

The 1988 FPLP Survey

The final, and perhaps most important, gauge of how far opinion leaders' attitudes had changed by 1988 comes from Holsti and Rosenau's FPLP survey, which was administered in March and April of that year. Their data corroborate the conclusion, based on more anecdotal information, that American opinion leaders had begun to reconsider their views about the Soviet Union, but, as yet, were still suspicious about Soviet motives and doubtful about the longevity of change.

On the one hand, many respondents were optimistic about Gorbachev and his reforms. Respondents were asked in 1988 whether "The Gorbachev regime in the USSR is sincerely seeking to stabilize relations with the United States," and 83 percent agreed (see table 2.1). Also, we can see evidence that opinion leaders—reacting to the warming of relations between the superpowers—had begun to downscale their perceptions of the threat posed by the Soviet Union. As table 2.2 shows, opinion leaders' concerns about Soviet military strength relative to the United States had dropped significantly between 1984 and 1988 (by seventeen percentage points), as had their concern about Soviet expansion into the Third World (by nine percentage points).

But, on the other hand, these respondents were still wary of Soviet intentions. The FPLP has repeatedly asked questions about Soviet foreign policy since the initiation of the study in 1976. As table 2.1 shows, 73 percent still believed in 1988 that the Soviet Union was "generally expansionist rather than defensive in its foreign policy goals," down only five percentage points from 1984. And while a somewhat smaller percentage of respondents than before displayed skepticism about détente—a significant minority (39 percent) still believed that it "permits the USSR to pursue policies that promote rather than restrain conflict." These data show that Gorbachev's ascension in the Soviet Union had caused only a small shift, but not a fundamental change, in attitudes within the United States by 1988.

The mixture of Americans' optimism and wariness is best seen in their reaction to the INF Treaty.[24] We see in table 2.3 that most respondents—83 percent—believed that the Senate should ratify the treaty without amendments. At the same time, 55 percent thought the

TABLE 2.1.   Leaders' Perceptions about Soviet Foreign Policy, 1976–88 (by percentage who agree)

Questions about Soviet Foreign Policy	Year			
	1976	1980	1984	1988
The Soviet Union is generally expansionist rather than defensive in its foreign policy goals	83	85	78	73
Détente permits the USSR to pursue policies that promote rather than restrain conflict	57	60	45	39
Revolutionary forces in Third World countries are usually nationalist rather than controlled by the USSR or China	60	58	68	73
Soviet foreign policy goals are inherently expansionist and will not change until there is a fundamental transformation of the Soviet system	*	*	69	62
The Soviet Union and the United States share a number of foreign policy interests such as prevention of war, arms control, and stabilizing relations between them	*	*	82	89
The Gorbachev regime in the USSR is sincerely seeking to stabilize relations with the United States	*	*	*	83

Source: Holsti 1990a. Reprinted with permission.
Note: Asterisks indicate that the question was not posed in that year.

**TABLE 2.2.   Leaders' Perceptions about the Greatest National Security Threats
Likely to Face the United States, 1980–88 (by percentage who checked each item)**

National Security Threats (Respondents chose two items)	Year		
	1980 (*n* = 2,502)	1984 (*n* = 2,515)	1988 (*n* = 2,226)
An increase of Soviet military strength relative to that of the United States	50	38	21
Soviet expansion into Third World areas	35	34	25
A growing gap between rich and poor nations	26	43	49
An inability to solve such domestic problems as the decay of cities, unemployment, inflation, racial conflict, and crime	50	39	61

Source: Holsti 1990a. Reprinted with permission.

**TABLE 2.3.   Leaders' Perceptions about the INF Treaty (by percentage
who agree)**

Questions about the INF Treaty	1988
The INF Treaty is in the interest of the West because it requires the Soviet Union to scrap more weapons than the United States	62
Although the INF Treaty includes stringent verification procedures, the Soviets are likely to violate it	55
The United States and its allies should build up NATO's conventional forces even if doing so requires increased taxes	56
Because the INF Treaty leaves the Soviets and their allies with a conventional force advantage in Europe, it is not in NATO's interest	29
The Senate should ratify the INF Treaty without amendments	83

Source: Holsti 1990a. Reprinted with permission.

Soviets were likely to violate the treaty, and 56 percent agreed that it was
necessary to build up NATO's conventional forces.

Summary

All three gauges of American elite opinion indicate that by the spring of
1988—when the first wave of the LOP study was administered—
relations between the superpowers had improved, but, as yet, the Cold
War was not perceived as over. According to the most optimistic assessment, Gorbachev was sincerely attempting to change Soviet foreign and

military policy; but the verdict was still out on whether other Soviet groups would rally behind Gorbachev and, therefore, on whether the Soviet reforms would actually lessen the military threat posed by that country. At this point in time, the pessimists could still argue that changes in the Soviet Union were only cosmetic and that "new thinking" was propaganda. American leaders' images of Russia had not changed substantially. Neither side of the political spectrum was ready to pronounce the Cold War over.

Gorbachev's UN Speech, December 1988

A month after Bush's electoral victory, Gorbachev offered the most important peace initiative to date. Speaking at the United Nations on December 7, 1988, Gorbachev unveiled a deep and unilateral cut in Soviet troops and conventional armaments.

Gorbachev began his speech by stating that the world had changed dramatically from what it had been earlier in the century. He described the emergence of a new interdependence and stated that no nation could develop normally outside the world economy. He argued that international relations needed to be freed from ideology. And he repudiated the use of force as an instrument of foreign policy (Oberdorfer 1991, 316–17).

Then, after speaking for forty-five minutes, Gorbachev announced that the Soviet Union had decided to unilaterally reduce its armed forces by 500,000 men, 10,000 tanks, 8,500 artillery systems, and 800 combat aircraft. Regarding Eastern Europe, he stated that six tank divisions would be withdrawn and disbanded from East Germany, Czechoslovakia, and Hungary. The Soviet troops in those countries were to be reduced by 50,000 men and their armaments by 5,000 tanks (Gorbachev 1988, A16).

"Soviet foreign policy had been shifting and turning for nearly all the forty-five months that Gorbachev had been in power," *Washington Post* reporter and author Don Oberdorfer (1991, 318) observed,

> but many millions of people in the West were still wary, disbelieving or not paying attention. Gorbachev's appearance at the United Nations, and especially the unilateral military cuts, was a dramatic moment of validation that the changes in Moscow's policy were vitally important and that they were real.

Almost a month later, a *New York Times* editorial urged President-elect George Bush to discuss the future of U.S. foreign policy in his inaugural address: "Most important," the editorial read, "he will need to respond to the visionary program for restructuring international relations that Mikhail Gorbachev outlined recently at the UN" (*New York Times* 1989a, E26).

The Bush Team and Its Critics, 1989

When Brent Scowcroft, the newly appointed national security advisor, was asked about Gorbachev's UN initiative during an interview on ABC's *This Week with David Brinkley,* he commented that "the Cold War is not over." Gorbachev "badly needs a period of stability," Scowcroft said, and is also "interested in making trouble within the Western alliance" using "a peace offensive."

> There may be, in the saying, light at the end of the tunnel. But I think it depends partly on how we behave whether the light is the sun or an incoming locomotive. (Hoffman 1989, A9)

Scowcroft's comments reflected the Bush administration's determination to proceed with caution. The foreign policy team that President Bush assembled was critical of the Reagan administration's "euphoric" reaction to the new Soviet leader. As one administration official put it, "The people appointed were refugees from the Ford administration with a mid-1970s outlook" who did not believe that anything had substantially changed within the Soviet Union.[25] Another official observed that "the Bush administration was not ready to deal with Gorbachev" at first: some "words were purposefully avoided" such as "cooperation," "the end of the Cold War," and "reduced threat."[26] Indeed, the first action that Bush took was to order an interagency review of changes within the Soviet Union—a process that delayed any public discussion of policy until April.

Two schools of thought emerged within the administration—what Thomas Friedman, a *New York Times* reporter, labeled the "hard-line skeptics" and the "pragmatic skeptics" (Friedman 1989b, A10). Vice President Dan Quayle, Deputy National Security Advisor Robert Gates, and Defense Secretary Richard Cheney all took the stance that Soviet reforms were bound to fail and that the future held prolonged conflict between the superpowers. For instance, Cheney told reporters in early April 1989 that he had become "a believer in the notion that Gorbachev wants fundamentally to reform Soviet society economically," but he warned that it was "risky business for us to make basic, fundamental changes in our own posture" (Wilson 1989, A12). "If I had to guess today," Cheney commented later that month during a CNN interview program hosted by conservatives Rowland Evans and Robert Novak,

> I would guess that [Gorbachev] would ultimately fail. . . . And when that happens, he's likely to be replaced by somebody who will be far more hostile than he's been in terms of his attitude towards the West. (Moore 1989, A17)

The White House distanced itself from this view (Devroy 1989, A15).

Robert Gates was even more openly pessimistic about the changes within the Soviet Union.[27] He stated in a public address in October 1988 that "Whether Gorbachev succeeds, fails, or just survives, a still long competition and struggle with the Soviet Union lie before us." Gates's position had not changed by April 1989: he argued, during a speech in Brussels, that past Soviet leaders had also tried to reform the Soviet system and their failure should make us skeptical of Gorbachev's chances. "Our view of the Soviet Union cannot be based on the personalities of its leaders," Gates stated, "but on the nature of the system itself" (Ignatius 1989, B2).[28]

President Bush and Secretary of State James Baker adopted a more moderate line. In May 1989, Baker, borrowing an idea from the Dukakis campaign, told reporters about a strategy of "testing" the Soviet leadership:

> We want to test the new thinking across the whole range of our relationship. *If* we find that the Soviet Union is serious about new global behavior, *then* we will seek diplomatic engagement in an effort to reach mutual beneficial results. (Beschloss and Talbott 1993, 59–60; emphasis in original)

The same month, Bush traveled to Texas A & M University to give a commencement speech that was billed as the president's declaration of his Soviet policy. Bush (1989, 700) stated that "containment worked" and

> now it was time to move beyond containment to a new policy for the 1990s, one that recognizes the full scope of change taking place around the world and in the Soviet Union itself.

He went on to declare a "sincere desire to see perestroika, this reform, continue and succeed." But, he added, American national security policy "is not predicated on hope. It must be based on deeds. And we look for enduring, ingrained economic and political change."

A similar debate was simmering within the intelligence community. One intelligence official remarked that Cheney was "spanked" for his statement that Gorbachev's tenure was limited, and that the leadership of the CIA's Office of Soviet Analysis (SOVA) held the "same analysis."[29] Indeed, Grey Hodnett, a senior political analyst in SOVA, wrote a paper in September entitled "Gorbachev's Domestic Gambles and Instability." In it, Hodnett argued that Gorbachev would be destroyed by the reforms he had unleashed or else he would try to save himself by returning to "old thinking" (Beschloss and Talbott 1993, 142). Hodnett's critique of Gorbachev was also endorsed by the director of SOVA, George Kolt, and by Fritz Ermarth of the National Intelligence Council. In general, the SOVA leadership "took the view that 'new thinking' wasn't real," and that "Gorbachev was embattled" and his "demise imminent." The implication of their analysis was that the administration should "limit involvement" with the Soviet leader.[30]

In contrast, Robert Blackwell, the CIA's national intelligence officer for the Soviet Union, wrote a paper with a more optimistic tone. Blackwell argued that 1990–91 would be a tumultuous time in the Soviet Union, but that Gorbachev would most likely be able to control events and to succeed. The Soviet leader may have to use tough measures, Blackwell predicted, but this would not derail reform (Beschloss and Talbott 1993, 141–42). This analysis implied that the administration should work with Gorbachev.[31]

By the spring of 1989, some members of the American establishment—outside the administration—began to believe that East-West relations had fundamentally changed. On April, 2, 1989, a *New York Times* editorial declared that "The Cold War is over" (*New York Times* 1989b, E30). Two days later, George Kennan, the man credited with the original enunciation of containment policy, testified before the Senate Foreign Relations Committee. He argued that "the system of power by which [Russia] has been held together and governed since 1917" was now breaking apart. "Fortunately," Kennan continued, "that breakup has been most pronounced in precisely those aspects of Soviet power that have been most troublesome" to our relations with that country: specifically, the "world revolutionary ideology, rhetoric, and political efforts" and the "morbid extremism of Stalinist political oppression." Most important, Kennan attacked the core of the old hard-line image as articulated in the NSC-68:

> In summary, it appears to me that whatever reasons there may once have been for regarding the Soviet Union primarily as a possible, if not probable, military opponent, the time for that sort of thing has

clearly passed. That country should now be regarded essentially as another great power like other great powers—one, that is, whose aspirations and policies are conditioned outstandingly by its own geographic situation, history, and tradition, and are therefore not identical with our own but are also not so seriously in conflict with ours as to justify any assumption that the outstanding differences could not be adjusted by the normal means of compromise and accommodation. (U.S. Congress 1989b, 12–13)[32]

Kennan concluded that now was the time to take a more positive approach to East-West relations.

Increasingly, the Bush administration was criticized for not seizing the opportunities presented by Gorbachev. On May 21, for example, the *New York Times* editorial was entitled "Take Me to Your Leader," and speculated that if aliens in a spaceship approached the earth with that message, we would be forced to take them to Gorbachev, not Bush (*New York Times* 1989c, E26). Later that month, just after Bush had finished his series of speeches billed as the results of the long-awaited policy review, the *New York Times* editorial was entitled "What East-West Policy?" Needless to say, the editorial writers were still not impressed: "President Bush yesterday delivered his fourth, final, flat and flimsy speech on East-West relations" (*New York Times* 1989d, A26). They chided the Bush team for their reticence to engage Gorbachev:

Mr. Bush and his key advisors are moderates. For most situations, that's a virtue. But in present circumstances, seeing different sides to every argument has become stifling. Their very moderation tends to blind them to the vast changes unfolding around the world, and to the power of language and bold goals.

In general, opinion leaders outside the administration began asking, in the words of Les Aspin, "Why isn't there any more 'seize the opportunity' in your thinking. . . . I mean, why not try and be a little more creative and more forthcoming when we make a proposal." Instead of setting up tests that the Soviets had to meet, "how about testing Gorbachev through proposing that we jointly solve some problem?" (U.S. Congress 1989a, 112).[33]

By September, Bush's cautious approach to the Soviet Union had become a heated partisan issue. In remarks made on the Senate floor, George Mitchell, Senate majority leader and Democrat from Maine, accused the Bush administration of having a "basic ambivalence" about Gorbachev and of being "nostalgic" about the Cold War.

This ambivalence is difficult to understand. . . . For over 40 years, the United States has demanded that the Soviet Union change its political system and loosen its stranglehold over the countries of Eastern Europe. The Western alliance, formed to confront the threat of Soviet totalitarianism, has consistently urged the Soviet Union to decentralize its political and economic system and grant every citizen the right to speak, to worship, to emigrate freely.

What we have demanded for over four decades is beginning to occur. . . . Now is the time for the United States to encourage and capitalize upon the changes we have sought for so long. Instead of encouragement and engagement, the Administration has adopted an almost passive stance. (Friedman 1989a, A1, A14)

In the face of growing criticism, Baker decided that it was time for a more positive and assertive policy toward the Soviet Union. "In August of 1989," one administration official remembered, "Baker made a conscious decision to be the pointman" on relations with the Soviet Union.[34] Baker had come to trust Shevardnadze, the Soviet foreign minister, especially after their retreat to his ranch in Wyoming in September. Also, unless the administration rose above its skepticism of the Soviet leader "we," as Baker told associates, "will be hung out to dry." He believed that the Republican Party would be hurt in 1992, NATO allies would go their own way, and Bush would be remembered as the president who missed the opportunity to end the Cold War (Friedman 1989b, A10).

Baker went public with a new approach in October 1989. He gave two speeches stating that the administration wanted perestroika to succeed and that the two countries should respond to this "historic opportunity" to end the Cold War by searching for "points of mutual advantage" (Oberdorfer 1989a, A16).[35] Gates had also written a speech to be given that month: he argued that lasting reform within the Soviet Union was unlikely because it would have to overcome seventy-two years of communism and a millennium of Russian history, and that Gorbachev was not trying to establish a new system but attempting to repair the old one (Beschloss and Talbott 1993, 124). After Gates sent the speech to the State Department for review, Baker called Scowcroft and asked him to cancel it (Oberdorfer 1989b, A18). Gates's speech was quashed.

The End of the Cold War

In 1968, the Soviet Union sent in tanks to oust Czech reformers, and Brezhnev enunciated the doctrine that bore his name: he claimed that the

Soviet Union had the right to send in armed forces to assist any communist government in jeopardy. Twenty-one years later, on October 25, 1989, Gennadi Gerasimov, a spokesperson for the Soviet Foreign Ministry, publicly stated that the "Brezhnev Doctrine is dead." In its place, he joked, "We now have the Sinatra doctrine. You know the Frank Sinatra song 'My Way'? Hungary and Poland are doing it their way" (Oberdorfer 1991, 355; see also Beschloss and Talbott 1993, 134). And, indeed, in the late summer and fall of 1989, it became clear to the world that the Soviet Union would no longer exert military force to ensure that communist governments ruled the nations of Eastern Europe.

Between August and November of 1989, the political balance in Europe was transformed. First, the communists within Poland conceded control over the government to leaders of the Solidarity movement. Gorbachev, in a telephone conversation with Mieczyslaw Rakowski, the Polish general secretary, apparently encouraged him to cooperate in this transference of power to a noncommunist-led government (Oberdorfer 1991, 360–61).

Then, Gorbachev stood aside and allowed the Berlin Wall to be dismantled.[36] In response to signs of turmoil in East Germany, Gorbachev ordered his General Staff to make sure that Soviet troops did not get involved (Beschloss and Talbott 1993, 133). Without Soviet backing, Erich Honecker, the East German communist leader, ordered security forces to quash demonstrations that were erupting in several cities. Egon Krenz, the security chief, refused, and allowed tens of thousands of people to march in Leipzig on October 9. Although Honecker was forced to resign by the politburo on October 18, the public protests kept mounting. On October 25, Gorbachev, while in Helsinki, stated publicly that the Soviet Union had "no right, moral or political" to interfere in the events unfolding in Eastern Europe and that "We assume others will not interfere, either" (Beschloss and Talbott 1993, 134). Ten days later, 500,000 people demonstrated in East Berlin. Krenz reportedly called Gorbachev and was advised that the border between the two Germanys should be opened to serve as a proverbial escape valve, to release political steam (Oberdorfer 1991, 363; Beschloss and Talbott 1993, 134). By November 9, the crossing points between East and West Germany were opened, and jubilant crowds from each side gathered to celebrate and to demolish the wall.

"No one" within the American intelligence community foresaw the Soviets "walking out of Eastern Europe" and "permitting non-communist governments to come to power."[37] To the West, these events signaled the sincerity of Gorbachev's intentions and, simultaneously, a decrease in the will and capability of the Soviet leadership to use military power beyond its borders. The new governments soon demanded the withdrawal of Soviet troops from their countries. By mid-1990, the Soviet Union had even agreed upon an arrangement for the reunification of Germany within NATO.[38] As authors Michael Beschloss and Strobe Talbott (1993, 238) note,

> If there was a single point at which the Cold War ended, it was probably this, the moment when Gorbachev acceded to German unification within NATO.

West and East Germany were officially reunited on October 3, 1990, completing the transformation of Europe.

The change in American attitudes toward the Soviet Union was quick and decisive. Returning in January 1990 after a two-month recess, Sam Nunn, chairman of the Senate Armed Services Committee, said "We've seen the threat change on TV every night. . . . We'll be looking at this changed threat as the foundation on which we build the budget" (Wines 1990a, A11). The term *peace dividend* became the new catchphrase of the day. Testifying before the Defense Policy Panel, Norman Augustine, chairman and CEO of Martin Marietta, articulated his alarm for the future of the American defense industry:

> in the 30 days after the fall of the Berlin Wall . . . defense stocks fell, on the average, a percentage equal to the decline of the stock market as a whole in the month following the crash of 1929. (U.S. Congress 1990a, 236)

The Bush administration now acknowledged that relations with the Soviet Union were at a turning point. Bush met Gorbachev at Malta in December—a meeting that had been secretly planned since the summer. In a joint statement after the summit, Bush said, "We stand at the threshold of a brand new era of U.S.-Soviet relations." Gorbachev declared, "We stated, both of us, that the world leaves one epoch of the Cold War and enters another epoch" (Oberdorfer 1991, 383).[39] In the months following the collapse of the Berlin Wall, *Washington Post* reporter David Hoffman spoke with seven high-ranking officials: "Bush and his top policy-makers have undergone an important transformation in their thinking," he wrote. "They now accept Gorbachev as the engine of change and are seeking to exploit his enthusiasm for reform, rather than wait for it to fail" (Hoffman 1990, 11). Ed Hewett, a Soviet specialist who had advised Bush and later was appointed to the National Security Council (NSC), said:

the administration didn't want to believe its own eyes and ears. Over time, it became hard to do. You had to have your head in some deep sand by the end of last year [1989]. The watershed event was East Germany and the Berlin Wall. . . . For us, that was an event that changed the whole paradigm, the way we think about Soviet foreign policy. We realized the wall came down because he [Gorbachev] put his foot on it and shoved it. (Hoffman 1990, 11)

Cheney continued to portray the Soviet Union as a threat, but his behavior was interpreted by others as an attempt to fend off budget cuts. The defense secretary's 1990 budget proposal stated on the first page that reductions in Soviet military capabilities were "still relatively easy to reverse" and that the United States "must be prepared to remain in long-term competition" with the Soviet Union (Wines 1990b, A1, A13). Cheney also initially clung to the old fourteen-day warning-time scenario for a Soviet attack on Europe, despite an earlier report (representing the views of the JCS, the CIA, and the Defense Intelligence Agency [DIA]) that the Soviet Union had been incapable of such quick mobilization for the past several years (see Tyler 1989, A1; Tyler 1990, 31; Moore and Tyler 1990, 6–7).

At the same time, William Webster, the director of the CIA, testified before Nunn's committee that it was now unlikely that the Soviet Union would pose a conventional threat to the United States in the foreseeable future. Webster recognized the vulnerability of Gorbachev but said that

even if a hardline regime were able to retain power in Moscow, it would have little incentive to engage in major confrontations with the United States. New leaders would be largely preoccupied with the country's urgent domestic problems, and would be unlikely to indulge in a major military buildup.

As a result, a successor regime would face the same types of economic and political pressures that President Gorbachev has, and would probably continue to pursue arms control agreements with the West. . . . In closing, Mr. Chairman, even a major reversal of leadership and policies in Moscow would be unlikely to restore an international order resembling the one that existed until only a few years ago. (Webster 1990)

By this time, then, the CIA had perceived that a profound weakness in the Soviet economy would inhibit future Soviet foreign policy; some criticized the agency for not recognizing this flaw within the Soviet system much earlier.[40] Cheney, reacting to Webster's testimony, admitted in a television interview that

> there's no question but what it would be easier for me, in terms of getting Congressional approval of the budget that the President sent up [if] there were a little more restraint in [Webster's] statements. (Wicker 1990, A25)

The 1990 CCFR Survey Results

The sea change in opinion leaders' attitudes following the collapse of the Berlin Wall was evident in the 1990 Chicago Council on Foreign Relations (CCFR) survey. Again, like the FPLP, the CCFR is a trend study of American opinion leaders. The CCFR has sampled opinion leaders every four years since 1974; the FPLP every four years since 1976. (See appendix B for a discussion of the differences between trend data and panel data.)

By mid-autumn 1990, a strong majority—73 percent—of the CCFR elite respondents believed that the Cold War was over.[41] Only 20 percent considered the "military power of the Soviet Union" as a "critical" threat to the United States, whereas 63 percent considered the "economic power of Japan" to be so. Only 8 percent thought that the Soviet Union would be the "main adversary of the United States" during the next ten years, whereas 17 percent chose Japan and 27 percent chose Iraq (Rielly 1991b). These numbers alone suggest that American opinion leaders' perceptions of the Soviet Union had undergone a fundamental change.

The previous CCFR survey, conducted in 1986, provides a benchmark from which to judge the precipitous opinion change that had occurred by 1990. As table 2.4 shows, in 1986, only 28 percent of elite

TABLE 2.4. Leaders' Perceptions about the U.S.-Soviet Military Balance, 1982–90 (in percentages)

	Year		
Military Balance	1982	1986	1990
U.S. stronger	20	28	71
About equal	62	59	26
USSR stronger	15	11	3
Don't know	3	2	0

Source: Chicago Council on Foreign Relations. Data available through ICPSR.
Note: Percentages may not total one hundred due to rounding.

respondents thought that the United States was "stronger in terms of military power" than the Soviet Union, and 59 percent thought that the two countries were about equal. By 1990, 71 percent perceived the United States as stronger, 26 percent thought the two countries were equal, and a mere 3 percent still believed that the Soviet Union was stronger.

CCFR data on opinion leaders' attitudes toward NATO and defense spending reveal the same pattern. As table 2.5 shows, in 1986, 77 percent of CCFR respondents thought that the U.S. commitment to NATO should be kept the same, and only 14 percent believed it should be decreased or withdrawn entirely. But by 1990, after the fall of the Berlin Wall, 35 percent believed that the U.S. commitment should be kept the same, whereas a majority—61 percent—now believed it could be lessened. Likewise, as shown in table 2.6, in 1986, 48 percent of elite respondents thought that defense spending should be cut back; this number swelled to 77 percent by 1990.[42]

TABLE 2.5. Leaders' Commitment to NATO, 1986–90 (in percentages)

	Year	
U.S. Commitment to NATO	1986	1990
Increase commitment	8	3
Keep commitment as it is	77	35
Decrease our commitment	13	57
Withdraw entirely	1	4
Not sure	1	1

Source: Chicago Council on Foreign Relations, 1986 and 1990. Data available through the ICPSR.

TABLE 2.6. Leaders' Opinions on U.S. Defense Spending, 1986–90 (in percentages)

	Year	
Defense Spending	1986	1990
Expand	11	2
Keep same	37	20
Cut back	48	77
Don't know	3	0

Source: Chicago Council on Foreign Relations, 1986 and 1990. Data available through the ICPSR.

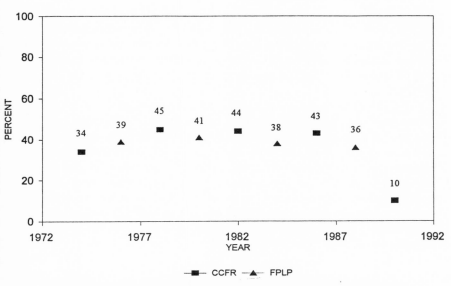

Fig. 2.1. Leaders' attitudes toward the goal of containing Communism, percentage who chose "very important." (Data from ICPSR and Holsti 1990a.)

One series of questions has been asked repeatedly by both the FPLP and the CCFR (and was also included on the LOP questionnaire); it enables us to pinpoint more precisely when attitudes about the Soviet threat fundamentally changed. More specifically, both survey houses asked respondents to evaluate the importance of various foreign policy goals. As shown in figure 2.1, a significant minority—between 34 and 45 percent—of respondents in both studies consistently believed that "containing communism" was a "very important" foreign policy goal. The FPLP data show that the percentage of respondents who chose this response option dropped from 38 percent in 1984 to 36 percent in 1988—a difference of only two percentage points. Such a small difference could be attributable to sampling error; that is, it may not actually reflect an opinion change at all. In contrast, CCFR data shows a sharp drop from 43 percent in 1986 to 10 percent in 1990—a difference of thirty-three points.

Likewise, we can see in figure 2.2 that the percentage of FPLP respondents that considered "matching Soviet power" a "very important" foreign policy goal dropped from 40 percent in 1984 to 32 percent in 1988—a difference of eight percentage points. The percentage of CCFR respondents who chose that response option dropped from 59 percent in 1986 to 20 percent in 1990—a difference of thirty-nine percentage points.

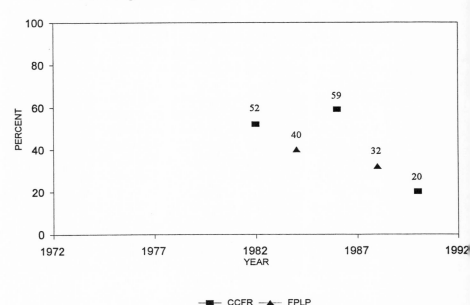

Fig. 2.2. Leaders' attitudes toward the goal of matching Soviet power, percentage who chose "very important." (Data from ICPSR and Holsti 1990a.)

These data support the anecdotal account, detailed earlier, that the turning point in elite opinion occurred after the revolutions in Eastern Europe. As described earlier, the FPLP trend data had shown that by 1988 elites were optimistic about Gorbachev's reforms but still wary of Soviet intentions. We see here again that the FPLP trend data do not reveal a sharp change in opinion leaders' attitudes by 1988 toward the importance of "containing communism" or "matching Soviet power." The CCFR data, in contrast, reveal that a profound change in opinion had occurred by 1990.

Final Act: The Collapse of the Soviet Union

Some conservatives did continue to perceive the Soviet Union through Cold War lenses.[43] Within the government, the leadership (not the rank and file) of the CIA's SOVA remained highly suspicious of Gorbachev.[44] But the position that the Soviet threat was undiminished or that the Cold War was unabated was decidedly a minority view that lacked credibility.

After all, in July 1991, the Warsaw Pact Treaty Organization was dissolved. Soviet military forces had withdrawn from Czechoslovakia and Hungary and were in the process of withdrawing from Germany and Poland (Garthoff 1994, 465). In August, after the coup attempt against Gorbachev, Boris Yeltsin, president of the Russian Republic, banned the Communist Party of the Soviet Union, after seventy-four years in power (Garthoff 1994, 478–80).

The CPD was one organization that "stuck to [its] knitting" to the bitter end. As late as August 1991, its message remained the same (although its staff, membership, and resources had dwindled considerably). The CPD spokesperson still argued that "Military power has continued to shift in favor of the Soviets." "The Cold War may not be over," the public relations official continued, "they have not disappeared as a military threat."[45]

Only a few months later, the Soviet Union ceased to exist. On December 8, 1991, the leaders of Russia, Belorussia, and the Ukraine publicly announced the formation of the "Commonwealth of Independent States." A little over two weeks later, on Christmas day, Gorbachev resigned as president of the USSR. Even the CPD had disbanded by the following summer.[46]

LOP Panel Results, 1988–92

Several months after the dissolution of the Soviet Union—in the spring of 1992—the second wave of the LOP study was administered. By that time, the Cold War had been over for about two years. As demonstrated earlier, a precipitous change in opinion had occurred by 1990. Not surprisingly, then, the LOP data capture the transformation in opinion leaders' images regarding Russia and containment policy.

Tables 2.7 and 2.8 show conclusively the the LOP respondents revised their perceptions about the foreign policy motivations of Russia. In 1988, respondents were asked whether "the Soviet Union is generally expansionist rather than defensive in its foreign policy goals" and most—421 out of 586—had agreed.[47] In 1992, they were asked whether "Once their economic crisis stabilizes, Russia will become an expansionist military power." This time, however, only 20 percent of the 421 people who had agreed in 1988 that the Soviet Union was expansionist still thought in 1992 that Russia had expansionist tendencies; fully 80 percent had changed their minds between the two waves of the panel study (see table 2.7). And the change in opinions is almost entirely unidirectional: 93 percent of the 165 people who had disagreed in 1988 that the Soviet Union was expansionist gave the same answer when asked a similar question about Russia in 1992; the other 7 percent are probably indicative of random measurement error. (See table B.1 in

TABLE 2.7.   Leaders' Changing Attitudes about the Expansionist Nature of the Soviet Union in 1988 and Russia in 1992, Turnover Table (in percentages)

		TIME 1 Soviet Union Expansionist, 1988 (Columns)		
		Agree	Disagree	Total
TIME 2 Russia Expansionist, 1992 (Rows)	Agree	20	7	17
	Disagree	80	93	83
	Total	100%	100%	100%
	N	421	165	586

Source: LOP panel data.
Note: See appendix B for a discussion of how to read a turnover table.

TABLE 2.8.   Leaders' Changing Attitudes about the Marxist Nature of the Soviet Union in 1988 and Russia in 1992, Turnover Table (in percentages)

		TIME 1 Soviet Union Marxist, 1988 (Columns)		
		Agree	Disagree	Total
TIME 2 Russia Marxist, 1992 (Rows)	Agree	24	11	19
	Disagree	76	89	81
	Total	100%	100%	100%
	N	371	222	593

Source: LOP panel data.
Note: See appendix B for a discussion of how to read a turnover table.

appendix B for a discussion about how to interpret data within turnover tables.)

We see the same pattern in table 2.8. In 1988, respondents were asked whether "Soviet foreign policy is essentially guided by Marxist-Leninist ideology" and most—371 out of 593—had agreed. In 1992, they were asked whether "Recent changes notwithstanding, Russian foreign and domestic policy is essentially guided by Marxist-Leninist ideology." This time only 24 percent of the 371 people who had thought that Soviet foreign policy was "Marxist-Leninist" in 1988 still thought the same about Russian policy by 1992; 76 percent had changed their views (see table 2.8). And almost all—89 percent—of the 222 people who had disagreed in 1988 that Soviet foreign policy was essentially guided by "Marxist-Leninist ideology" gave the same answer when asked in 1992.

Table 2.9 illustrates a similar sea change in attitudes about the policy of containing communism. Respondents were asked "how much importance" they thought should be attached to the goal of "containing communism" first in 1988 and again in 1992. Of the 216 people who in 1988 had thought the goal to be "very important," only 23 percent felt the same way by 1992; 55 percent had downgraded the goal to "somewhat important" and 23 percent thought it to be "not important at all." Again, the change in attitudes is unidirectional: almost all (94 percent) of the 95 people who in 1988 had considered containment not to be an important goal felt the same way by 1992.

American opinion leaders also reassessed specific military policies that had been established to counter or contain Soviet power. For instance, they were asked whether "the United States should bring home all its troops stationed in Europe" in both 1988 and 1992. In 1988, only 20 percent of respondents agreed with this strongly worded statement; this percentage grew to 47 percent by 1992. Further, as shown in table 2.10, almost 40 percent of those respondents who had disagreed with this statement in 1988 changed their positions by 1992. Likewise, respondents

TABLE 2.9. Leaders' Changing Attitudes between 1988 and 1992 about the Importance of Containing Communism, Turnover Table (in percentages)

		TIME 1 (Columns) 1988			
		Very	Somewhat	Not	Total
TIME 2 (Rows) 1992	Very	23	3	0	9
	Somewhat	55	33	6	37
	Not	23	64	94	54
	Total	100%	100%	100%	100%
	N	216	314	95	625

Source: LOP panel data.

Note: Percentages may not total one hundred due to rounding; see appendix B for a discussion of how to read a turnover table.

perceived "defending our allies' security" as a less important goal in 1992 than in 1988. Of those who had considered this goal to be "very important" in 1988, more than half—58 percent—attributed it less importance by 1992 (see table 2.11; note that the column percentages in the "not important" category should not be given much credence, because the number of individuals involved is so low). These findings suggest that many opinion leaders were reevaluating the U.S. role in Europe; however, attitude change on this issue may appear less pronounced than on others because new rationales, such as guarding against "instability," had emerged to justify a continued American presence.

By 1992, an overwhelming majority of the LOP respondents agreed

TABLE 2.10. Leaders' Attitudes over Time about Stationing Troops in Europe, 1988–92, Turnover Table (in percentages)

		TIME 1 Bring Troops Home, 1988 (Columns)		
TIME 2		Agree	Disagree	Total
Bring Troops Home, 1992	Agree	81	39	47
(Rows)	Disagree	19	61	53
	Total	100%	100%	100%
	N	126	504	630

Source: LOP panel data.
Note: See appendix B for a discussion of how to read a turnover table.

TABLE 2.11. Leaders' Attitudes over Time about the Importance of Defending Our Allies' Security, 1988–92, Turnover Table (in percentages)

		TIME 1 (Columns) 1988			
TIME 2		Very	Somewhat	Not	Total
(Rows) 1992	Very	42	13	0	26
	Somewhat	55	76	45	66
	Not	3	11	55	8
	Total	100%	100%	100%	100%
	N	305	322	11	638

Source: LOP panel data.
Note: See appendix B for a discussion of how to read a turnover table.

TABLE 2.12.   Leaders' Attitudes over Time about Defense Spending, 1988–92, Turnover Table (in percentages)

| | | TIME 1 Reduce Spending, 1988 (Columns) | | |
		Agree	Disagree	Total
TIME 2 Defense Spending Policy, 1992 (Rows)	Increase	0	4	1
	Keep Same	4	16	8
	Decrease	96	80	91
	Total	100%	100%	100%
	N	418	210	628

Source: LOP panel data.
Note: See appendix B for a discussion of how to read a turnover table.

that defense spending needed to be cut. Respondents were asked in 1988 about "Reducing the defense budget in order to increase the federal education budget": 67 percent agreed with this statement. It appears, then, that sentiment about reducing the defense budget preceded the end of the Cold War. However, that sentiment later swelled into a consensus. Respondents were asked in the second wave whether defense spending "should be increased, kept about the same, or decreased." Over 90 percent believed it should be cut back. Moreover, 80 percent of those respondents who in 1988 were against reducing the defense budget had changed their positions by 1992 (table 2.12).

The LOP panel data show unambiguously that respondents' perceptions about Russia and containment had changed by 1992, and that they had adjusted their views on related policy issues as well.

Conclusion

The aim of this chapter has been to place the LOP panel study within a broader political context and to demonstrate that the Cold War ended in the interim between waves. Although Mikhail Gorbachev came to power in March 1985 and began to initiate reforms soon thereafter, it took several years for American opinion leaders to shed their familiar suspicions about Soviet motivations. In 1988—when the first wave of the LOP panel study was administered—most American leaders remained wary of Soviet foreign policy intentions. Relations between the superpowers had improved remarkably, but the Cold War was not yet over. The revolutions in Eastern Europe in 1989 and the reunification of

Germany in 1990 were the culminating events that fundamentally shifted Americans' perceptions about the threat posed by the Soviet Union. This sea change in elite opinion was evident in the CCFR 1990 poll. Hence, by the time the second wave of the LOP panel was administered, in the spring of 1992, leaders' images regarding Russia and their attitudes about containment policy had already been transformed. In short, the LOP study successfully captures opinion leaders' foreign policy views from the time periods before and after the end of the Cold War.

Now we can turn our attention to the question of what other foreign policy attitudes were affected by the Soviet collapse. Did the end of the Cold War provoke American opinion leaders to recast their most basic foreign policy orientations?

CHAPTER 3

Continuity in Opinion Leaders' Foreign Policy Postures

The purpose of this chapter is to demonstrate that leaders' basic foreign policy postures (defined as militant and cooperative internationalism) were not buffeted by the end of the Cold War. Knowledge about the depth of leaders' reactions, in turn, provides a clue about the structure of their belief systems: it tells us something about the linkages between these postures and other beliefs. We shall see, for instance, that these postures were not "functionally related" to or "constrained" by perceptions about the Soviet Union.

The analysis used here will build on two distinct analytical approaches within the literature on foreign policy beliefs. The first uses exploratory factor analysis to uncover the broad organizing dimensions underlying Americans' opinions. The findings provide us with descriptive information about people's general foreign policy postures.

By demonstrating that basic postures remained stable despite the end of the Cold War, we will also test a theory embedded within a second analytical approach. Scholars had posited a causal relationship between Americans' images of their main adversary—the Soviet Union—and their other foreign policy beliefs (Hurwitz and Peffley 1990; Peffley and Hurwitz 1992; see also Herrmann 1986; Koopman, Snyder, and Jervis 1989, 1990). We have already seen signs of "dynamic constraint" between leaders' images of the Soviet Union and directly related issues, such as containment or defense spending. In this chapter, however, I will show that such dynamic constraint did not extend to some of the respondents' most basic foreign policy postures.

The chapter is organized as follows. The first section describes the research within these two analytical approaches. The second explains more explicitly how the argument here builds upon this past work. The third, using other elite panel studies, provides a rough benchmark from which to judge the stability in leaders' attitudes over time, and the fourth presents the Leadership Opinion Project (LOP) panel findings.

Past Research on Americans' Foreign Policy Beliefs

Descriptions of Belief Structure

Numerous scholars have focused on the structure of Americans' foreign policy beliefs since the Vietnam War.[1] Some scholars contested Almond's (1950) and Converse's (1964) unfavorable portrait of mass political opinions as flighty and inconsistent, searching out the hidden organizing principles that provided coherence within Americans' belief systems (Bardes and Oldendick 1978; Hurwitz and Peffley 1987, 1990; Wittkopf 1990; Peffley and Hurwitz 1992). Meanwhile, other scholars sought to categorize the competing "belief types" that together had created the political discord evident after the Vietnam War (Mandelbaum and Schneider 1979; Holsti and Rosenau 1984; Wittkopf 1990). Both enterprises required an investigation of the dimensions underlying Americans' foreign policy beliefs.

Scholars agreed that neither the traditional isolationism/internationalism continuum by itself, nor the liberal/conservative continuum, adequately characterized the spectrum of Americans' foreign policy beliefs in the post-Vietnam era. They identified multiple dimensions using exploratory factor analysis on survey data (Bardes and Oldendick 1978; Mandelbaum and Schneider 1979; Wittkopf 1990; Chittick and Billingsley 1989). While the exact number of identifiable dimensions was open to dispute,[2] most authors conceded that at least two distinctions were necessary to characterize Americans' beliefs: (1) whether the United States should be involved with the rest of the world and (2) if involvement is advocated, whether U.S. actions should be cooperative or militaristic (e.g., Mandelbaum and Schneider 1979; Wittkopf 1990; Holsti and Rosenau 1990).

For instance, Mandelbaum and Schneider (1979), using the 1974 Chicago Council on Foreign Relations (CCFR) data on the mass public, applied factor analysis to sixteen questions about the importance of various foreign policy goals, and found two different types of internationalism: one oriented toward cooperative relations with other countries and one oriented toward more competitive, militaristic, and interventionist goals.[3] From this finding, they concluded that Americans' foreign policy attitudes are bidimensional:

> It is appropriate to think of foreign policy attitudes as arrayed along two dimensions, an internationalist-isolationist dimension (*whether* the United States should play an active role in world affairs) and a cross-cutting liberal-conservative dimension (*what*

kind of role it should play). (Mandelbaum and Schneider 1979, 41; emphasis in original)

They then categorized the American people into three belief types:

> *Conservative internationalists* had positive scores on internationalism and interventionism; they represent the strongest supporters of the cold-war internationalist consensus. *Liberal internationalists* had positive scores on internationalism but *not* on interventionism; they represent the new variety of internationalism that has emerged in the post-Vietnam era, one that rejects militaristic and interventionist values but continues to favor an active U.S. role in the world. The residual category, those with negative scores on the internationalism factor, were labeled simply *noninternationalists.* (42–43; emphasis in original)

Noninternationalists, they noted, could also be divided into liberals and conservatives.[4]

Holsti and Rosenau (1984, 1986) derived a similar trichotomy—which they named the "Three-Headed Eagle"—from their Foreign Policy Leadership Project (FPLP) data on American opinion leaders.[5] Using their 1976 and 1980 FPLP trend data, Holsti and Rosenau investigated the impact of the Vietnam War on leaders' foreign policy beliefs: whether the breakdown of consensus was accompanied by the formation of new, competing belief systems. They distributed respondents into seven groups based upon their answers to two questions: the first asked respondents to remember whether they had supported "complete victory," "complete withdrawal," or "something in between" when the war first became an issue; and the second asked whether they had held the same view at the end of the war.[6] Holsti and Rosenau then compared the respondents within these groups across a wide variety of questions about the nature of the international system and the appropriate U.S. role in the world, and identified three coherent belief types: "Cold War Internationalists," "Post–Cold War Internationalists," and "Semi-Isolationists."

The "Three-Headed Eagle" identified by Holsti and Rosenau was quite similar to the three belief clusters reported by Mandelbaum and Schneider. In both analyses, one group exhibited militaristic and security concerns (viewing the world primarily in East-West terms); another placed humanitarian, economic, and cooperative goals as priorities in U.S. foreign policy; and a third preferred less involvement with the world. The major substantive distinction between these two analyses was that Mandelbaum and Schneider classified a respondent as belonging to a particular belief type by using his or her placement on two dimensions (i.e., liberalism/conservatism and isolationism/internationalism), whereas Holsti and Rosenau did not. Their omission engendered some debate about whether Holsti and Rosenau's identified belief types were in fact three separate dimensions (Chittick and Billingsley 1989) or whether they too could be located across two dimensions (Wittkopf 1986).[7]

Wittkopf (sometimes with others) reinterpreted the CCFR trend data and refined the basic schematic representation of Americans' beliefs detailed earlier (Wittkopf 1981, 1986, 1990; Maggiotto and Wittkopf 1981; Wittkopf and Maggiotto 1983a, 1983b).[8] He also found that two main factors structured Americans' foreign policy beliefs. From this information, however, Wittkopf did not conceptualize people's beliefs as defined by two cross-cutting dimensions with one axis labeled liberalism/conservatism and the other isolationism/internationalism, as was done earlier by Mandelbaum and Schneider. Rather, he conceived of one axis as militant internationalism (MI) and the other as cooperative internationalism (CI). This scheme yielded *four* belief types: hardliners (support MI and oppose CI), accommodationists (support CI and oppose MI), internationalists (support both MI and CI), and isolationists (oppose both MI and CI).[9]

In a movement toward consensus, Holsti and Rosenau (1990) then applied Wittkopf's scheme to their 1976, 1980, and 1984 FPLP data. "If the militant internationalism and cooperative internationalism are indeed basic," they reasoned,

> in the sense that they are necessary if not sufficient to describe beliefs about international affairs, then the four types derived from these two dimensions should differ significantly and systematically in their responses to a broad range of questions other than those used to define the MI and CI dimensions. . . . Stated somewhat differently, can we discern in the [FPLP] data a hierarchy of beliefs about international affairs in which responses to militant and cooperative internationalism are central and predictive of responses to a broad range of other questions? (97)

Whereas "Wittkopf generated superordinate dimensions inductively from exploratory factor analyses of correlations between specific attitudes," Holsti and Rosenau "measured the dimensions directly" (1990, 121).[10] In other words, they used the description of the factors found by Wittkopf, and measured militant and cooperative internationalism with appropriate question items.[11] They used the two resultant scales to group respondents into the four belief types discovered by Wittkopf, and then compared the different groups' answers to a wide variety of questions. Despite some questions about the applicability of the isolationist category to their elite samples, Holsti and Rosenau concluded that

> The evidence presented here, combined with Wittkopf's findings from the four CCFR surveys, suggests that the MI and CI dimensions are very strong contenders for describing superordinate beliefs, or core beliefs if the appropriate metaphor is a circle rather than a pyramid, that are causally linked to others. Placement on these two dimensions appears to provide strong clues as to how one thinks about a broad range of other issues. (122)

The "MI/CI classification scheme," they added, had "survived a demanding series of tests" (122).

But did the "MI/CI scheme" survive the end of the Cold War? Once the Cold War ended, scholars refocused their attention onto the question of whether these research findings were time-bound (Holsti 1992). There has already been some *indirect evidence* that these dimensions continue to structure Americans' foreign policy beliefs. Wittkopf (1994, 384) extended his previous analysis to the 1990 CCFR data—a transitional period during which the Cold War was ending—and found

> striking continuity with the past when similar analytical procedures are followed. The foreign policy thinking of elites and masses continues to be characterized by two internationalism dimensions.

In addition, Holsti and Rosenau (1993) analyzed their 1992 FPLP data to see whether militant and cooperative internationalism persisted as central beliefs in the post–Cold War era. They used the same technique as before (1990), although they had to adjust the question items for the MI dimension somewhat.[12] They concluded that

> On balance, the 1992 leadership survey evidence indicates that positions on militant and cooperative internationalism, yielding four distinct types, continue to provide an effective way of organising attitudes on a broad range of issues. (Holsti and Rosenau 1993, 249)

But much more direct and compelling evidence can be obtained with panel data (see appendix B). Trend data can only compare the aggregate results from different samples over time; they cannot track belief changes at the individual level. Hence, these analyses about the continued importance of the MI/CI dimensions can only *presume* that individuals' stances toward these dimensions remained stable over time. But opinion analysts know that stability at the aggregate level does not necessarily translate into stability at the individual level: if roughly equal numbers of people change positions in opposite directions they can cancel each other out (and become hidden) at the aggregate level. Only panel data can confirm attitude stability at the individual level over time.

Also, with the LOP panel data, we have information about respondents' past beliefs, and, when addressing research questions about attitude change, this is an important advantage. Holsti and Rosenau (1993, 237), due to the nature of their data, were forced to measure respondents' positions on the MI/CI dimensions in 1992, and then assess whether these dimensions provided "a powerful predictor" for individuals' attitudes toward "a broad array of international issues" as also measured at the same time. Put differently, they created scales to measure 1992 belief constructs and then investigated whether these constructs predicted other 1992 attitudes: this endeavor was undertaken to show that the "fundamental structure of opinions" found before the end of the Cold War persists (236). Because their analysis of the 1992 FPLP sample yielded similar results to their analysis of the 1988 FPLP sample, they concluded that the basic structure of opinion leaders' belief systems had not changed. But it is more direct and convincing to track the same individuals over time, comparing their beliefs before and after the end of the Cold War.

Using the LOP panel study, I will measure individuals' 1988 stances toward the use of military force and toward cooperative efforts abroad, and then observe whether these postures had changed by 1992. By doing so, I will also address the question of whether "dynamic constraint" existed between respondents' images of the Soviet Union and their MI/CI postures.

The Centrality of Attitudes about the Soviet Union

A second analytic approach treated Americans' images of the Soviet Union as a key variable that structured other attitudes. At the most descriptive level, analysts provided typologies of the various assumptions Americans made about the nature of the Soviet Union and the policy recommendations that flowed from those assumptions (e.g., Yergin 1977; Dallin and Lapidus 1983; Herrmann 1985; Tetlock 1983). Going further, some scholars argued that American leaders (Herrmann 1986; Koopman, Snyder, and Jervis 1989, 1990) and citizens (Hurwitz and Peffley 1990; Peffley and Hurwitz 1992) relied upon Soviet schemas to simplify the complexities of international affairs.

Koopman, Snyder, and Jervis (1989, 1990), for instance, "examined the extent to which people's responses to a postulated international crisis are influenced by their beliefs, especially beliefs about the Soviet Union" (1989, 121). In 1986, they asked a sample of subscribers to *International Security* for their views about the Soviet Union and for their policy recommendations to a hypothetical Persian Gulf crisis. The authors randomly divided the respondents into groups; each group received questionnaires with a different version of the crisis scenario. "This allowed us," the authors argued, "to determine the relative impact of general beliefs about international politics and the Soviet Union as compared to detailed differences in the situation" (1990, 695). And they found that the former mattered much more than the latter: "General beliefs about an adversary's motives and about the importance of demonstrating resolve [were] . . . particularly good predictors of advocating military actions in response to the scenario" (1990, 716). But while this research implied that American leaders' preconceptions about the Soviet Union constrained other beliefs, these authors did not discuss the range of issues or attitudes to which the Soviet "schema" might have been applied.

Herrmann (1986) addressed this issue more directly. He investigated "whether or not leaders generalize from a basic 'Soviet schema' " (841) and if they apply a "common framework" across "a number of arenas and in particular across different regions of the Third World" (843).[13] He speculated that, in the case of Americans,

> the general view of the Soviet Union may represent a fundamental construction of reality in which policy choices are made and subproblems defined. The basic understanding of the global strategic situation may operate as if it were a schema "filling in" the specifics for regional situations that are hard to decipher. If this is so, it ought to affect foreign policy choices across a broad range of issues. (844)

To test this hypothesis, Herrmann (using the 1986 CCFR elite data) created an index to measure a "Soviet-containment schema" and then correlated this index with thirty-four policy-related questions. The policy questions were quite diverse, addressing issues within seven areas: (1) Latin America, (2) the Middle East, (3) Asia, (4) Africa, (5) Western Europe, (6) direct relations with the USSR, and (7) nuclear weapons. Although not equally useful in all areas, Herrmann found that the

Soviet-containment schema was "clearly related to many policy decisions and . . . more strongly associated with these choices than a number of commonly used variables" (869) such as party identification or ideological self-identification.[14]

Hurwitz and Peffley (1987, 1990) went much further. They argued that people's images of the Soviet Union were causally prior both to their foreign policy postures and to many policy preferences. More specifically, they argued that

> individuals rely on *postures*—or, broad, abstract beliefs regarding the general direction the government should take in international affairs—to constrain more specific policy attitudes in a top-down fashion. (1990, 4; emphasis in original)

Citizens' images of the Soviet Union, in turn, were "superordinate" to such postures as militarism, isolationism, or containment (1990, 5). In sum, these authors posited that

> beliefs about the basic nature of the Soviet Union operate as central premises in mass belief systems in foreign affairs, both by constraining general foreign policy postures and by shaping more specific preferences on national security issues.[15] (1990, 22)

As partial corroboration for their model, Peffley and Hurwitz (1992) investigated how people reacted to the warmer relationship exhibited by Gorbachev and Reagan between 1987 and 1988. Using mass panel data, they found that as respondents revised their images of the Soviet Union, their attitudes on *specific policy issues* also moved in a "dovish" direction.[16] (For alternative views, see Bartels 1994 and Sulfaro 1994.)

This particular finding is in accordance with the evidence presented in chapter 2. We saw there, for instance, that opinion leaders' attitudes about defense spending changed once the Cold War ended, as did their attitudes on containment. But it is hardly surprising to find that people's opinions about specific military policies—which had been established and justified as a means of countering Soviet military strength—changed once the Soviet Union collapsed. Such attitude change might alternatively be explained as a simple recognition of a new objective reality or as evidence that people possessed Soviet schemas with a range that encompassed directly related national security policies.

The additional question of whether dynamic constraint existed between people's changing images of Russia and their *general postures* has not yet been tested with either mass or elite data. If Hurwitz and Peffley's (1990) model was accurate, then we would expect to find that people's basic postures changed once the Soviet Union collapsed. Respondents' attitudes about the use of military force, for instance, should move in a dovish direction as their perceptions about Russia soften. The end of the Cold War allows us to test this model (at least for opinion leaders) using the LOP panel data; we can disentangle, for the first time, whether leaders' basic postures, such as their general attitudes about the use of military force, were derived from evaluations about the threat posed by a longtime adversary.

A Post–Cold War Research Strategy

Before proceeding, we must define what leaders' basic postures toward international affairs were before the end of the Cold War. Only then can we investigate the dynamic relationship between these postures and leaders' changing images of Russia.

The solution lies in what have we learned about the structure of Americans' foreign policy beliefs from the factor analytic literature. Factor analysis "refers to a variety of statistical techniques whose common objective is to represent a set of variables in terms of a smaller number of hypothetical variables" (Kim and Mueller 1978, 9). For our purposes, the larger set of variables consists of people's responses to individual question items, primarily about foreign policy issues, in a particular survey. As we have seen, various analysts used this technique to ascertain the dimensions that organize attitudes about foreign policy.[17] They analyzed a variety of data sets, administered in different years, by different survey houses, using different questionnaires.[18] Yet, different analysts came up with similar findings (Bardes and Oldendick 1978; Mandelbaum and Schneider 1979; Wittkopf 1990; Chittick and Billingsley 1989; see also Holsti and Rosenau 1990, 98; Herrmann 1986, 852). Two factors (and sometimes others) consistently emerged from exploratory factor analyses on people's foreign policy opinions: one factor was described by question items about the use of military force and interventionist politics and the other by question items about cooperative efforts to solve international problems and to help other countries. Equally important, these findings make sense given what we know about the public debate on foreign policy: even when leaders agree that the United States should be involved in the world, they do not agree about the goals that should be pursued or the tactics used.[19] Herein lies my rationale for defining leaders' basic postures as their stances toward militant and cooperative internationalism.[20]

If the two factors that Wittkopf (and others) have identified are meaningful, then analysts should be able to measure these dimensions directly with appropriate questions. As noted earlier, Holsti and Rosenau (1990, 1993) take this approach. Following their lead, I am able to create reliable scales to measure leaders' 1988 and 1992 attitudes about the use of military instruments of power and about U.S. involvement in cooperative efforts with other countries (see appendix C).

Although I use the labels *cooperative internationalism* and *military internationalism* to describe these attitude constructs, it is important to note that this choice is somewhat arbitrary; similar factors could be, and are, given other labels by other scholars. For instance, Bardes and Oldendick use the label *militarism* to describe a factor on which questions about military commitments, military strength, national security, the protection of weak nations, the defense of allies, and the containment of communism all load highly. And they use the label *world problems* to describe a factor on which questions about helping less-developed countries, pursuing arms control, combating world hunger, fostering international cooperation, and keeping peace all load highly. Again, these factors are quite similar to those described by Wittkopf and by Holsti and Rosenau as MI and CI.[21]

And, despite adopting the CI/MI labels, I conceptualize these attitude constructs somewhat differently than others. To begin with, in the various factor analyses reported earlier, the militant internationalism dimension (or its equivalent by a different label) was characterized by questions regarding the use of military force and the containment of communism.[22] We would now expect, however, that respondents' views on the Soviet Union and containment would change simply because the object has changed: the Soviet Union no longer exists; its containment is no longer relevant. We would expect respondents to recognize these changes, and indeed we already know that they did by the evidence presented in chapter 2. The question under investigation here is whether the respondents' more general orientations toward international affairs—in this case, their attitudes about the projection of American military force abroad—have changed as well. Therefore, I separated the core elements of militant internationalism and used two pairs of scales to measure the stability and change of this dimension. The first pair (COMM88, COMM92) taps respondents' beliefs about the containment of communism in 1988 and 1992. The second pair (MI88, MI92) taps respondents' more general beliefs about the use of military instruments of power before and after the end of the Cold War. (See table C.1 in appendix C for the question items used to create these indexes.)

Most important, I treat the CI and MI factors as *separate attitude constructs* (thereby loosening assumptions about how they are related to each other), and investigate how *each* of these factors is linked with other beliefs. This is something of a departure from earlier approaches: Wittkopf (1990, 1994) and Holsti and Rosenau (1990, 1993) conceptualize the MI/CI factors as *two orthogonal dimensions* and use them to classify people into four belief types.[23] They then describe how these different *types* of people (that is, "hard-liners," "accommodationists," "internationalists," and "isolationists") answer other questions.[24] But they do not look at how each of these attitude constructs *per se* is interlinked with other beliefs.

In contrast, I explore the interrelationship between each of these factors and respondents' images of the Soviet Union. (I will also explore the interrelationship between these factors and other variables in chapter 4.) I will show that leaders' images about Russia did change between 1988 and 1992, but each of these basic postures remained quite stable. The implication, then, is that leaders' images of the Soviet Union did not serve to constrain basic postures as posited.

Methodological Considerations

Two methodological issues must be addressed briefly before we can use the LOP panel data to evaluate the stability of leaders' foreign policy postures between 1988 and 1992: (1) how can we measure attitude stability using panel data? (2) what are realistic benchmarks for assessing stability using survey data within an elite sample?

One method for measuring the stability of attitudes over time combines the Pearson product moment correlation coefficient and a mean-difference score. The correlation coefficient measures the stability of individual positioning between the two waves; but it "taps the stability of *relative* individual positions across a population, not absolute ones" (Converse and Markus 1979, 37; emphasis in original). While a low correlation indicates substantial shifting by respondents between waves, a high correlation does not necessarily imply stability between waves—only stability in the relative placement of individuals. If many people change response options all together, and if they do so without "leapfrogging" each other, the correlation over time will be high. So, we need another criterion besides the Pearson r to assess stability: the mean-difference score tells us whether such a tide shift in attitudes has taken place.

The second issue that must be addressed concerns the interpretation of the correlation coefficient. At what point is this statistic too low to be considered as evidence of attitude stability over time? There are several explanations for why individuals choose different response options when presented with the same questions at two different points in time. The fluctuation may reflect genuine opinion change.[25] But it could also be an indication of "nonattitudes" on the part of some respondents (Converse 1964) or of random measurement error that arises from the survey instrument itself (Achen 1975).[26] Even among an elite sample, not all respondents will have formed an opinion on every question, and some degree of random measurement error must also be expected.[27] Therefore, it is highly unlikely that a particular elite sample would fill out the same questionnaire at two different times in exactly the same manner, even if genuine attitude change does not occur. We need to assess, short of a perfect interwave correlation, what amount of fluctuation constitutes attitude stability within a sample. We need to find a standard, a rough benchmark.

The most obvious place to look is at the findings in past panel studies. There is ample data on the stability, or lack thereof, of mass beliefs. For instance, Jennings and Niemi (1978, 338), "somewhat arbitrarily," to use their own words, "establish values of .3 [tau-*b* correlation] or higher as demonstrating substantial persistence" in mass attitudes over an eight-year period.[28]

However, it is not clear that we should expect an elite sample to yield similar results. Past research provides mixed signals regarding this question. On the one hand, Converse (1964) assumed that an elite sample would exhibit greater attitude stability than a mass sample but provided no longitudinal evidence to support this hypothesis.[29] On the other hand, Achen (1975) implies that elite and mass samples would not be much different (at least once corrected for random measurement error) given that both are exposed to a fallible measurement instrument.[30] More recently, Jennings (1992) compared the interwave correlations of mass and elite samples on identical questions. He found that the elite samples—delegates to the Republican and Democratic national conventions—exhibited consistently higher interwave correlations than the mass samples.[31]

Perhaps, then, we should consider only elite panel studies. One problem is that such studies are rare: I have found only two articles that report correlation coefficients over time for a reasonably sized elite sample.[32] A second problem is that the sampling procedures, the question items used, the time interval between waves, and other variables are all different: the findings from these studies can only be seen as a rough standard.

Jennings (1992) reports interwave correlations for three panel studies with delegates to the national party conventions as participants. The first panel study was conducted between 1972–80, the second between 1980–84, and the third between 1984–88. The latter two studies provide a better comparison with the LOP study in terms of the time period between waves—that is, four years rather than eight years. Also, Jennings reports interwave correlations for several different kinds of questions: for example, respondents' feelings toward different sociological groups, their feelings toward "highly visible party leaders," as well as their attitudes toward particular social issues (Jennings 1992, 427). Other studies have shown, using mass data, that not all questions yield the same interwave correlation coefficients: questions about party attachments tend to be highest, followed next by questions about likes and dislikes of prominent political leaders, whereas questions about policy issues tend to be lower (Converse and Markus, 1979). Although none of these questions serve as a direct comparison with the more general orientations about the role of government in international affairs tapped by the MI and CI scales, policy issues are perhaps the closest. In brief, the most appropriate benchmarks from Jennings's study are as follows: the average correlation over time for issue positions—abortion, busing, and defense spending—was .72 in the 1980–84 panel and .81 in the 1984–88 panel (see table 3.1).

The other elite panel study, conducted by Putnam, Leonardi, and Nanetti (1979) included ninety-five Italian regional politicians.[33] Despite the nationality difference, I believe this study provides a better comparison because the authors used multiple-item scales to measure respondents' more general orientations toward politics over time. Their results are displayed in table 3.2. The interwave correlations for two scales— their "Left-Right Issues Index" and their "Index of Alienation from Pluralist Politics"—were especially high at .85 and .83.[34] The "Political Elitism Index" and the "Index of Opposition to Central Government" garnered somewhat lower correlations over time at .57 and .60, respectively.[35] From these results, Putnam and his colleagues concluded that their elite respondents had stable beliefs:

> Their ideological commitments . . . their attitudes toward democratic institutions . . . and some aspects of their attitudes toward Italian regionalism are shown to be remarkably stable over time. (1979, 463)

Together, these studies provide a rough standard by which to judge the interwave correlations within elite panel studies. Another benchmark for attitude stability can be derived from the LOP panel itself. We can reasonably assume that questions about domestic policies would not

TABLE 3.1. Rough Benchmark of Elite Attitude Stability: Delegates to National Party Conventions, Pearson Coefficients over Time

Topics of Questions	Delegate Panel Studies		
	1	2	3
Issues:			
Abortion	N/A	0.75	0.82
Busing	N/A	0.79	0.80
Defense spending	N/A	0.62	0.80
Average	N/A	0.72	0.81
Groups:			
Union leaders	0.56	0.80	0.84
Business interests	0.56	0.63	0.61
Women's movement	0.68	0.79	0.85
Blacks	0.60	0.68	0.71
Conservatives	0.75	0.87	0.88
Liberals	0.81	0.87	0.88
Republicans	0.74	0.88	0.90
Democrats	0.74	0.88	0.90
Average	0.68	0.80	0.82
Leaders:			
R. Nixon	0.74	0.79	N/A
T. Kennedy	0.77	0.89	0.87
G. McGovern	0.81	0.82	N/A
G. Ford	N/A	0.68	0.71
Average	0.77	0.80	0.79

Source: M. Kent Jennings. "Ideological Thinking among Mass Publics and Political Elites." *Public Opinion Quarterly* 56 (1992): 440. Reprinted by permission of the University of Chicago Press.

Note: The first panel study was conducted between 1972 and 1980, the second between 1980 and 1984, and the third between 1984 and 1988.

TABLE 3.2. Rough Benchmark of Elite Attitude Stability: Italian Regional Politicians, Pearson Coefficients over Time

Name of Scale	Pearson *r*
Left/right issues index	0.85
Index of alienation from pluralist politics	0.83
Political elitism index	0.57
Index of opposition to central government	0.60

Source: Robert Putnam, Robert Leonardi, and Raffaella Y. Nanetti. 1979. "Attitude Stability among Italian Elites." *American Journal of Political Science* 23, no. 3: 478, 483, 485. Reprinted by permission of The University of Wisconsin Press.

be influenced much by changes in the international environment, and we know that politics at home were not unusually turbulent between 1988 and 1992. Hence, I also include a domestic policy index within my analysis for comparison.[36]

LOP Panel Findings

We are now prepared to assess how stable leaders' beliefs were once the Cold War ended. Table 3.3 presents the interwave correlation coefficients and mean-difference scores for scales measuring domestic policy stances (DOM88, DOM92), militant internationalism (MI88, MI92), cooperative internationalism (CI88, CI92), attitudes toward containment policy (COMM88, COMM92), and perceptions about the expansionist motivations of the Soviet Union and Russia (SU88, RUS92). Appendix C details how the indexes were constructed as well as their reliability.

Let us first consider the stability over time of respondents' attitudes toward domestic policy, as this provides a rough benchmark by which to judge the other indexes. We see that the interwave correlation coefficient for DOM88 and DOM92 is quite high at .86.[37] (Notice that this is the same correlation over time reported by Putnam, Leonardi, and Nanetti for their Right/Left Index on domestic issues. See table 3.2.) At the same time, the mean-difference score is minuscule: .01 on a one-point scale.[38]

The results from the domestic indexes, then, along with past panel

TABLE 3.3.   Stability in Leaders' Beliefs over Time, 1988 and 1992

Type of Belief	Pearson *r*	Change in Means
Domestic policy		
[DOM88, DOM92]	0.86	0.01
Militant internationalism		
[MI88, MI92]	0.72	0.04
Containment		
[COMM88, COMM92]	0.74	−0.16
Cooperative internationalism		
[CI88, CI92]	0.69	0.02
Images of USSR-Russia		
[SU88, RUS92]	0.39	−0.21
N = 660		

Source: LOP panel data.

Note: All of the mean-difference scores are statistically significant at the .05 level. Negative values in mean score indicate movement in a liberal direction.

studies, constitute a standard by which to assess continuity or change in leaders' foreign policy beliefs. We can see that respondents' more general orientations toward the use of force abroad and cooperative internationalism pass the test. To begin with, the interwave Pearson *r* for MI88 and MI92 is strong at .72 (notice that this correlation over time is higher than some reported by Putnam, Leonardi, and Nanetti. See table 3.2).[39] Also, the mean moved only slightly—at .04—and in the conservative direction, that is, toward greater support for the use of force. Not only is the mean-difference score quite small, but the shift is in the opposite direction than would be expected had this posture been constrained by perceptions about the Soviet Union.[40] Likewise, respondents' stances toward cooperative internationalism also remained quite stable. The interwave coefficient for CI88 and CI92 is again high at .69 and the mean-difference score is small at .02.[41]

We also find considerable continuity—although not stability—in leaders' attitudes about the containment of communism. The Pearson *r* between COMM88 and COMM92 was very strong at .74; this shows that respondents' beliefs in 1988 are quite predictive of their beliefs in 1992.[42] At the same time, however, the movement in the mean is much more substantial at −.16. Together, these findings demonstrate that leaders have all moved together toward the view that containment is less important.[43]

Last, the evidence suggests much change, and indeed confusion, in leaders' perceptions about Russia. Leaders' views about Soviet expansionist motivations as measured in 1988 (SU88) are only moderately associated with their concerns about Russian expansionist tendencies as measured in 1992 (RUS92). The interwave correlation coefficient—at .39—is low judging by our rough benchmarks, indicating substantial shifting of positions between waves.[44] It is possible that the correlation coefficient was deflated because, unlike the other scales, SU88 and RUS92 were derived from similar but not identical questions. Because the Soviet Union collapsed, it was impossible to use repeated questions to measure leaders' perceptions of that country over time. Still, the relatively low interwave correlation is quite suggestive: leaders' beliefs about the Soviet Union-Russia reveal much less continuity, which, considering the profound transformation that occurred within Russia between 1988 and 1992, only makes sense. And although leaders shifted their positions about Russia in a disorderly fashion (i.e., by leapfrogging each other), there still was a sea change in perceptions: the mean-difference score is quite substantial—at −.21—indicating that leaders dramatically softened their perceptions about the expansionist motivations of Russia.[45]

Overall, then, the evidence shows that leaders' images of Russia changed profoundly between 1988 and 1992, and that they reassessed their views about the policy of containment. Yet leaders' general stances toward cooperative internationalism and militant internationalism stayed quite stable, suggesting that leaders' images of the Soviet Union did not constrain these postures. We can further corroborate this evidence by examining, more directly, the dynamic relationship between attitudes as revealed by individual question items; we can see whether individuals who change their views on one question item also change their views on another question item.

Let us consider, for example, whether respondents who softened their views about the Soviet Union-Russia also reconsidered their views about the importance of U.S. military power. Using the 1988 panel wave, I selected only those respondents who agreed that the "Soviet Union is generally expansionist" and who also considered the "military superiority of the United States" to be either a "very effective" or a "moderately effective" approach to world peace (see table C.1 for exact question wordings). Out of the 307 respondents selected, 240 (78 percent) changed their views about Russia by 1992, no longer believing that country to be "an expansionist military power." But most of those who changed their views about Russia *did not* change their views about the utility of military power: out of these 240 respondents, 196 (82 percent) still believed in the effectiveness of U.S. military power as an approach to world peace by 1992.[46]

In contrast, we do find evidence of dynamic constraint in respondents' evaluations about the importance of containment. In this instance, I selected only those respondents who agreed in 1988 that the Soviet Union was expansionist and who also believed that "containing communism" was a "very important" foreign policy goal. Out of 174 respondents, 123 (71 percent) revised their views about Russia by 1992 and most changed their views about containment as well. Only 25 (20 percent) of these 123 respondents still considered containment to be "very important" in 1992; 98 (80 percent) had downgraded this goal to be only "somewhat important" or "not at all important."

Conclusion

The collapse of the Soviet Union allows analysts to determine whether certain variables—people's images of an adversary and their foreign policy postures—are "functionally related." Except for attitudes toward containment policy, the data presented here demonstrate that they are not. Leaders' images of Russia and their attitudes about containment policy have changed; but some of their basic orientations toward the international arena—their attitudes about the use of military force abroad and about U.S. engagement in cooperative activities with other countries—remained quite stable between 1988 and 1992. In other words, the evidence demonstrates that there was no dynamic constraint between leaders' images of the Soviet Union and their MI/CI postures.

If we had found that respondents' basic foreign policy orientations had changed between 1988 and 1992, we would have concluded that leaders' images of the Soviet Union had structured these beliefs. What, then, does the continuity of these postures tell us about the structure of elite beliefs? At least two alternative explanations are consistent with this finding:

1. *Lag time:* Images of the Soviet Union did constrain leaders' for-eign policy postures during the Cold War, but there is a lag time between the collapse of the Soviet Union and the adjustment of foreign policy postures. In short, the causal process has not fully worked itself out yet.
2. *Other Sources of Foreign Policy Postures:* Images of the Soviet Union were not the most important source of constraint for leaders' foreign policy postures. Other variables structure these beliefs.

A categorical refutation of the first explanation is beyond the scope of the LOP data (it would require a third wave), but there are several reasons to strongly doubt its validity. While it is true that the Soviet Union officially ceased to exist only a few months before the 1992 ques-tionnaire was sent out, the process of deterioration within the Soviet Union had been evident for a long time. Jervis (1976) observes that beliefs, while normally resistant to change, are most vulnerable when contradictory information is received dramatically and in large batches. Such a process began as early as the fall of 1989 with an event of enor-mous symbolic and geopolitical importance—the widely reported dis-mantling of the Berlin Wall—and continued at rapid pace thereafter. In other words, respondents had more than two years to work through the implications of the end of the Cold War for their other beliefs.

Further, the adjustment process was swift for some issues. We have seen here that leaders did change their views on containment policy as they reevaluated Russia, and they also adjusted their views on some security policies, such as defense spending. Why, then, would some attitudes that were constrained by leaders' images of the Soviet Union change and others not? Why would it take respondents longer to work through the implications of the Soviet collapse for some beliefs than for others? It would appear that some attitudes were directly linked to perceptions about the Soviet Union, while others were not.

The second explanation points to the need for further investigation into the sources of foreign policy postures. Some scholars have postulated a causal association between people's core values and their foreign policy preferences (Rokeach 1973; Lumsdaine 1992). And authors who have studied elite beliefs after the Vietnam War have found an association between domestic and foreign policy beliefs (Russett and Hanson 1975; Schneider 1979; Holsti and Rosenau 1988; Holsti 1994). It is conceivable, then, that leaders' domestic ideological orientations and core values—variables that did not change en masse with the disintegration of the Soviet Union—anchored their responses to the end of the Cold War. A consideration of these alternative variables will be the subject of the next chapter.

CHAPTER 4

The Structure of Opinion Leaders' Foreign Policy Beliefs

Why would opinion leaders' foreign policy postures remain stable even within the context of profound international change? What does this finding tell us about the structure of elite beliefs? The aim of this chapter is to consider whether other variables—besides respondents' images of the Soviet Union—might have constrained their foreign policy postures. I will argue that leaders' more general stances toward militant and cooperative internationalism are derived from, and bound together with, their core values and ideological orientations, and that these latter variables anchored their responses to the end of the Cold War.

The chapter is organized as follows. The first section demonstrates constraint over time between respondents' domestic views and their foreign policy postures. The second section posits an explanatory framework, arguing that both types of beliefs—that is, foreign policy postures and domestic ideological orientations—may be derived from a common source, namely, core values. It is possible that opinion leaders apply the same or kindred values to policy issues within both policy domains, and that different attitudes are tied together by ideology into cognitive packages. The third section addresses a side issue raised by these findings: how should we characterize the dimensionality of elite beliefs? If domestic and foreign policy beliefs are closely interconnected, does that mean that elite beliefs are unidimensional, organized along a liberal-to-conservative continuum?

Linkages between Domestic and Foreign Policy Beliefs

The recent literature on leaders' foreign policy beliefs acknowledges that these beliefs are linked to domestic attitudes, but, in general, does not incorporate this relationship into an explanatory framework. Scholars have tended to approach elite belief systems in a manner almost undifferentiated from analyses of mass beliefs—even though the two groups inherently provoke different research agendas—and thereby have downplayed the interconnectedness between foreign policy and domestic beliefs.

To be more specific, much of the academic debate on the structure of beliefs was provoked by Converse (1964). He argued that elites and the mass public possess different kinds of belief systems. Elites organize their beliefs according to a few abstract and widely shared principles, such as liberalism and conservatism. The mass public, on the other hand, is "innocent of 'ideology' ": its beliefs are scattered, unorganized, and idiosyncratic (1964, 241).[1] With regard to the mass public, then, the discovery of organization among beliefs, in and of itself, was a contribution to the literature and had important normative implications for democratic theory.[2] Taking up this research agenda, Bardes and Oldendick (1978) and Wittkopf (1981, 1990), among others, used exploratory factor analysis on survey data, and found that the foreign policy beliefs of the mass public were organized along several broad dimensions. Mass beliefs are structured, they found, just not along the liberal-to-conservative dimension. In fact, the organizing dimensions for foreign policy attitudes were unique to that domain. For example, Wittkopf's (1990, 340) analysis demonstrated "unambiguously that the mass of the American people maintain highly structured foreign policy beliefs"; but at the same time "the nature of the conjuncture of their foreign and domestic policy beliefs" remained "unanswered."

Likewise, Hurwitz and Peffley (1987, 1990) concluded that mass beliefs on foreign policy were structured by a "domain-specific" heuristic.[3] Citizens organized their foreign policy beliefs according to a general and abstract principle—namely, their beliefs about the nature of the Soviet Union.[4] The common task of these authors was to locate structure within mass beliefs, and they all found organizing principles that were only relevant to foreign policy issues.

Similar approaches have been used to analyze leaders' foreign policy attitudes: scholars have tended toward domain-specific descriptions of the dimensions underlying opinion leaders' foreign policy beliefs; they have tended to downplay the interrelationships between foreign policy and domestic beliefs. Wittkopf and Maggiotto (1983a) and Wittkopf (1990), for instance, detailed how two dimensions—militant internationalism (MI) and cooperative internationalism (CI)—organize both mass and elite beliefs in that domain. Holsti and Rosenau (1990) later replicated these findings and showed that the foreign policy beliefs of their elite Foreign Policy Leadership Project (FPLP) sample could be categorized using these two dimensions as well. Leaders' domestic beliefs, Holsti (1994) added, are structured along two *different* dimensions.[5] Together, these research findings imply that leaders' foreign policy attitudes exhibit their own internal structure, one that is relatively distinct from the organizing principles of domestic beliefs.

At the same time, these authors certainly acknowledge that, for leaders, beliefs about foreign and domestic policy are not unrelated. Wittkopf (1990), Holsti and Rosenau (1988), and Holsti (1994) have observed that the four belief types derived from the "MI/CI scheme"— that is, hard-liners, accommodationists, isolationists, and internationalists—overlap with domestic ideological types. "The hardliners and, to a lesser extent, the internationalists," Holsti and Rosenau observed (1988, 274) "tend to be domestic conservatives, whereas accommodationists are predominantly liberal on domestic policy." They concluded from opinion leaders' "responses to many domestic and foreign policy issues" that "[t]he dominant pattern that emerges . . . is one of overlapping rather than cross-cutting cleavages, and the divisions are systematically correlated to a conventional conservative-to-liberal dimension" (1988, 277). Likewise, Wittkopf wrote that

> Partisanship and ideology both go a long way in explaining the differences in leaders' . . . foreign policy beliefs. Republicans and liberals are most consistent in their views, with the former embracing hardline values and the latter accommodationist values throughout the post-Vietnam era. Similarly, conservatives tend toward hardline values and Democrats toward internationalist values or accommodationist values. (1990, 132)

To sum up, these authors treat leaders' foreign policy attitudes as a distinct belief system with its own internal structure, but acknowledge that it overlaps with domestic ideological orientations.[6]

I will argue, in contrast, that opinion leaders' foreign policy postures and their domestic policy views are elements within the same belief configuration. Unlike some previous research, I do not presume that militant and cooperative internationalism are orthogonal dimensions. Accordingly, I do not use the two dimensions to generate four belief types and then explore the overlaps between these foreign policy *types* (e.g., hard-liners, accommodationists, isolationists, and internationalists) and domestic ideological groups (e.g., liberals and conservatives). Rather, I treat respondents' more general stances toward militant and cooperative internationalism as distinct belief constructs—and then investigate whether these constructs themselves are related to each other and to other variables. I find (1) that these two postures are substantially correlated with each other, (2) that each of them is even more highly correlated with domestic ideology, and, most important, (3) that the constraint between respondents' domestic ideological orientations and these foreign policy postures remains strong over time. In other words, by breaking down the artificial barrier between domestic and international affairs, we can account for the stability over time in opinion leaders' foreign policy postures.

Constraint across Domains over Time

Do opinion leaders possess belief structures that extend across policy domains? Did their domestic ideological orientations constrain their foreign policy postures before the end of the Cold War? Did such constraint anchor leaders' responses to the end of the Cold War? As I noted earlier, Converse (1964, 207) provides a useful definition of belief structure as "a configuration of ideas and attitudes in which the elements are bound together by some form of constraint or functional interdependence." Evidence of "constraint" or "functional interdependence," in turn, is "the success we would have in predicting, given initial knowledge that an individual holds a specific attitude, that he holds certain further ideas and attitudes."

Converse (1964), analyzing 1958 data, surmised that the foreign policy and domestic domains did constitute distinct belief systems. He compared responses from an elite population (congressional candidates in the 1958 off year elections) with a sample that represented the national electorate (the National Election Studies [NES] data). Table 4.1 shows the average correlation coefficients between question items for each group. As Converse reported,

The first thing the table conveys is the fact that, for both populations, there is some falling off of constraint *between* the domains of domestic and foreign policy, relative to the high level of constraint

TABLE 4.1.   Summary of Differences in Level of Constraint within and between Domains, Public and Elite, 1958

	Average Coefficients			
	Within Domestic Issues	Between Domestic and Foreign	Within Foreign Issues	Between Issues and Party
Elite	0.53	0.25	0.37	0.39
Mass	0.23	0.11	0.23	0.11

Source: Converse (1964, 229).
Note: Entries are tau-gamma coefficients.

within each domain. This result is to be expected: Such lowered values signify boundaries between belief systems that are relatively independent. (1964, 229; emphasis in original)

In short, even among leaders, the foreign and domestic policy domains were not part of the same belief configuration.

Thirty years later, the Leadership Opinion Project (LOP) panel data (like other studies conducted in the post-Vietnam era) tell a very different story. Tables 4.2 and 4.3 present correlation matrices for 1988 and 1992 data, respectively, and, in each instance, the evidence does

TABLE 4.2.   Constraint between Leaders' Foreign Policy and Domestic Beliefs, Pearson Coefficients, 1988

Indexes	IDEO88	DOM88	MI88	CI88	SU88
Ideology					
[IDEO88]	1.00				
Domestic policy					
[DOM88]	0.73	1.00			
Militant internationalism					
[MI88]	0.63	0.61	1.00		
Cooperative internationalism					
[CI88]	0.58	0.57	0.53	1.00	
Images of Soviet Union					
[SU88]	0.52	0.53	0.52	0.33	1.00

Source: LOP panel data.
Note: N = 660.

TABLE 4.3.   Constraint between Leaders' Foreign Policy and Domestic Beliefs, Pearson Coefficients, 1992

Indexes	IDEO92	DOM92	MI92	CI92	RUS92
Ideology					
[IDEO92]	1.00				
Domestic policy					
[DOM92]	0.78	1.00			
Militant internationalism					
[MI92]	0.51	0.56	1.00		
Cooperative internationalism					
[CI92]	0.44	0.51	0.41	1.00	
Images of Russia					
[RUS92]	0.34	0.34	0.26	0.27	1.00

Source: LOP panel data.
Note: N = 660.

suggest a "functional interdependence" between the two policy domains. Starting with the 1988 wave, notice first that the scales measuring militant (MI88) and cooperative internationalism (CI88) are substantially associated with each other ($r = .53$); and second, that each of these postures is even more strongly associated with domestic ideological orientations, whether measured by an ideological self-placement scale (IDEO88) or through questions about specific domestic policies (DOM88). For instance, the correlation between militant internationalism and domestic policy beliefs in 1988 was substantial at .61; and the correlation between cooperative internationalism and domestic beliefs was also strong at .57. This evidence indicates substantial constraint between the two policy domains within leaders' belief systems. (See appendix C for more information about the indexes.)

Furthermore, the strong interconnection between these beliefs outlived the Cold War (see table 4.3). The correlation between each of the foreign policy postures—militant internationalism (MI92) and cooperative internationalism (CI92)—and respondents' domestic policy views (DOM92) remained substantial in 1992 at .56 and .51, respectively.

Indeed, the panel data show across-wave constraint between these beliefs. Table 4.4 presents the correlations between respondents' ideological self-identification (IDEO88) and domestic policy preferences (DOM88) *as measured in 1988* and their general postures toward militant internationalism (MI92) and cooperative internationalism (CI92) *as measured four years later.* Respondents' preexisting domestic views, as measured by DOM88, are substantially associated with their post–Cold War foreign policy postures at .50 for militant internationalism and at .45 for cooperative internationalism. Together, this evidence suggests that these foreign policy postures are part of a larger belief system—

TABLE 4.4. Constraint over Time between Leaders' 1988 Domestic Beliefs and Their 1992 Foreign Policy Beliefs, Pearson Coefficients

Indexes	IDEO88	DOM88	MI92	CI92
Ideology [IDEO88]	1.00			
Domestic policy [DOM88]	0.73	1.00		
Militant internationalism [MI92]	0.52	0.50	1.00	
Cooperative internationalism [CI92]	0.47	0.45	0.41	1.00

Source: LOP panel data.
Note: N = 660.

extending across domains—that was largely immune to the events surrounding the end of the Cold War.

At the same time, we can see that the constraint between respondents' images of Russia and their other beliefs appears to have diminished sharply between 1988 and 1992 (tables 4.2 and 4.3). Before the end of the Cold War, leaders' perceptions about the nature and motivations of the Soviet Union (SU88) correlated highly with their domestic views ($r = .53$) and militant internationalism ($r = .52$), although more weakly with cooperative internationalism ($r = .33$). This suggests that leaders' beliefs about the nature of the Soviet Union were an element within this larger belief system before the end of the Cold War.

But apparently not a central element: by 1992, respondents' images about Russia had changed. As this "idea element" changed, however, respondents' other beliefs (at least those represented here), in both the domestic and foreign policy arenas, stayed quite stable. This might explain the diminished association between leaders' perceptions about Russia in 1992 (RUS92) and other measures: domestic policy preferences ($r = .34$) and militant internationalism ($r = .26$).[7]

In sum, these findings suggest that leaders' general foreign policy postures are elements within a larger belief structure, one that incorporates domestic ideological orientations as well. Further, as these postures remained stable over time—even as the external environment, and consequently, perceptions about Russia, changed—we can presume that they were constrained and anchored by domestic beliefs.

An Elaboration Model

In this section, my aim is to demonstrate that the association over time between respondents' foreign policy postures and their domestic views remains strong even when other variables are controlled. I incorporate four other independent variables. First, as I have already discussed, *images about the Soviet Union* must be considered as a potential source of beliefs (e.g., Hurwitz and Peffley 1990; Herrmann 1986). Second, *gender* is a variable commonly thought to influence attitudes about the use of military force (Brandes 1994; Holsti 1990c). Third, it seems plausible that *military service* could be an important socialization experience and might affect subsequent foreign policy beliefs. Fourth, some scholars have argued that *generational experiences*—the events that people experience as young adults—shape their subsequent orientations toward the international arena (Jervis 1976; Roskin 1974).[8] Appendix C describes the indexes used to measure these variables.

All the indexes used in the following regression analyses range between zero and one. This common scale allows us to compare the regression coefficients of the various independent variables and to assess their relative contribution.

Predicting Leaders' Foreign Policy Postures, 1988

Using the 1988 panel wave, table 4.5 presents the regression results for two equations. Equation (1) estimates respondents' stances toward militant internationalism; equation (2) estimates their stances toward cooperative internationalism.[9] Results from the first regression analysis show four variables as statistically significant at the .05 level: respondents' images of the Soviet Union, their gender, their membership in the Vietnam generation, and their domestic ideological orientations. Note, however, that the last variable possessed a much larger regression coefficient—at .44—than the others. This finding demonstrates the im-

TABLE 4.5.   Predicting Leaders' Foreign Policy Postures, Regression Results, 1988

Independent Variables	Dependent Variables	
	[1] MI	[2] CI
Constant	0.10	0.45
	(.02)	(.02)
Domestic views	0.44**	0.42**
	(.03)	(.03)
Military service	0.03	−0.02
	(.02)	(.02)
Gender	0.13**	0.06**
	(.02)	(.02)
Image of Soviet Union	0.29**	0.04
	(.03)	(.03)
Generation, WWII	0.01	0.05*
	(.03)	(.02)
Generation, Korea	0.03	0.03
	(.02)	(.02)
Generation, Vietnam	−0.04*	−0.01
	(.02)	(.02)
Adjusted r-squared	0.46	0.34
standard error	0.18	0.16
N	650	650

Source: LOP panel data.

Note: $*p < .05$, $**p < .01$. MI refers to militant internationalism, CI to cooperative internationalism. See table C.1 for question items used to construct these scales. The measurement of the independent variables is discussed in appendix B.

portance of domestic ideological orientations in estimating leaders' postures toward militant internationalism. If a respondent swung from the right end of the domestic ideological spectrum to the left end, then we would also expect an enormous change—.44 on a one-point scale—in that individual's orientation toward militant internationalism. Comparatively, the size of the regression coefficient for respondents' images about the Soviet Union was significantly smaller, at .29, while the other independent variables paled by comparison, at .13 for gender and .04 for membership in the Vietnam generation. Finally, we can see that this equation worked quite well by the standards of polling data: the adjusted *r*-squared was high, at .46.

Equation (2) shows similar findings for cooperative internationalism. In this instance, three independent variables are statistically significant at the .05 level: respondents' gender, their membership in the Second World War generation, and their domestic views. Once again, the regression coefficient for domestic views is quite large. If a respondent moved from one end of the domestic ideological spectrum to the other, we would expect a .42 change on the CI88 index. And, although the adjusted *r*-squared for this equation was lower, at .34, it is still quite respectable by the standards of survey research.

The results from these two regressions demonstrate that respondents' domestic ideological orientations were highly predictive of their foreign policy postures before the end of the Cold War.

Predicting Leaders' Foreign Policy Postures, 1992

Table 4.6 presents the regression results for four additional equations. Equation (3) estimates respondents' 1992 postures toward militant internationalism (MI92) using the same variables as before, except, of course, leaders' images of Russia (RUS92) substitute for their images of the Soviet Union.[10] We see again that domestic views possessed the largest regression coefficient at .46; this time, two other independent variables were statistically significant at the .05 level—images of Russia with a smaller coefficient of .10 and gender with a coefficient of .06.

Equation (4) also estimates 1992 stances toward militant internationalism, but an additional independent variable was added, namely, *respondents' past positions on militant internationalism (MI88)*.[11] Note that the inclusion of MI88 changed the regression results substantially; with a regression coefficient of .56, that variable became the best predictor of MI92 by far. The coefficient for domestic ideology dropped to .15, and the adjusted *r*-squared increased from .33 to .54. This does not suggest that domestic ideological orientation is a less important variable; only

TABLE 4.6. Predicting Elites' Foreign Policy Postures, Regression Results, 1992

Independent Variables	Dependent Variables			
	[3] MI	[4] MI	[5] CI	[6] CI
Constant	0.14	0.09	0.42	0.17
	(.03)	(.02)	(.03)	(.03)
Domestic views	0.46**	0.15**	0.36**	0.12**
	(.03)	(.03)	(.03)	(.03)
Military service	0.02	0.01	−0.01	0.01
	(.02)	(.02)	(.02)	(.01)
Gender	0.06*	−0.01	0.06**	0.03
	(.02)	(.02)	(.02)	(.02)
Image of Russia	0.10**	0.02	0.10**	0.05
	(.04)	(.03)	(.03)	(.03)
Generation, WWII	−0.03	−0.03	0.06*	0.04
	(.03)	(.02)	(.03)	(.02)
Generation, Korea	0.00	0.00	0.02	0.01
	(.02)	(.02)	(.02)	(.01)
Generation, Vietnam	−0.02	0.01	−0.02	−0.02
	(.02)	(.02)	(.02)	(.02)
Past MI posture [MI88]	N/A	0.56**	N/A	N/A
		(.03)		
Past CI posture [CI88]	N/A	N/A	N/A	0.58**
				(.04)
Adjusted r-squared	0.33	0.54	0.28	0.50
standard error	0.19	0.15	0.17	0.14
N	650	650	650	650

Source: LOP panel data.

Note: $*p < .05$, $**p < .01$. MI refers to militant internationalism, CI to cooperative internationalism. Equations (4) and (6) have the same dependent variables as equations (3) and (5), respectively, but one additional independent variable. See table C.1 for question items used to create the MI/CI scales and appendix B for a description of how the other variables were measured.

that it functions indirectly through MI88. In addition, the size of the MI88 coefficient adds further substantiation to earlier findings about the stability over time of this posture.

We see the same pattern with the other dependent variable, namely, respondents' stances toward cooperative internationalism in 1992 (CI92). Again, two equations were used: equation (5) uses the same independent variables as before; equation (6) adds respondents' past beliefs on this posture.[12] In the regression results for equation (5), we see again that domestic views had the largest coefficient at .36, followed by images of Russia at .10 and membership in the Second World War generation at .06. Note, in equation (6), that once respondents' past views of cooperative internationalism were included, CI88 garnered a coefficient of .58, and the adjusted *r*-squared rose from .28 to .50.

These additional regression results attest that respondents' foreign policy postures are bound together with and constrained by domestic beliefs. In each instance, domestic ideological orientation was the most powerful predictor of leaders' postures toward militant and cooperative internationalism. The only exceptions occurred when respondents' past beliefs on these postures were included in the regression; but, in those instances, we may presume that the respondents' past ideological orientations functioned indirectly. Moreover, the strength of past beliefs as predictors of more current beliefs reinforced our earlier findings on the continuities of opinion leaders' foreign policy postures.

Toward an Explanatory Framework

So far, the evidence has suggested that opinion leaders' general foreign policy postures and their domestic ideological orientations are both elements of the same belief structure. But what is the nature of the linkage between these different attitudes? Why do these variables exhibit constraint or "functional interdependence" with each other over time?

A reasonable conjecture—one that is consistent with the data here—is that respondents' foreign policy postures and their domestic ideological orientations are both expressions of common values. More simply, leaders may possess core values that inform preferences in both domains (Rokeach 1973). Lumsdaine (1992), for instance, argues that discrete values—toward aiding the poor or toward the use of force— influence people's attitudes about related issues without regard for domestic borders.[13] "The same principles and conclusions which people use in structuring and understanding other areas of life," Lumsdaine (1992, 9) explains, "are potentially applicable to international relations as well." He suggests several examples.

> For instance, it is reasonable to suppose that those who think that life's purposes are satisfied if they (and perhaps those personally close to them) survive and thrive, irrespective of what happens to others are unlikely to think that assistance to those abroad is an objective to support, unless strongly convinced that there are specific instrumental reasons for it. But those who think helping strangers a worthwhile activity in their own lives are more apt to think help to people overseas worthwhile. (1992, 9)

And another potential connection between domains, suggested by Lumsdaine (1992, 19), is through people's values about the use of force:

> A number of polls suggest that those who see the use of force (tough sentencing, the death penalty) as an effective way for government to control crime, and those opposed to gun control, tended to be more favorable toward the use of force to resolve international conflicts in Southeast Asia.

At first glance, the LOP data offer support for these hypotheses.[14] Regarding assistance to the poor, two policy questions were asked on the LOP questionnaires—one about domestic policy and one about foreign policy—that we can reasonably assume reflect this value: respondents were asked whether they agreed with "redistributing income from the wealthy to the poor through taxation and subsidies" and whether "the United States should give economic aid to poorer countries even if it means higher prices at home." And, as Lumsdaine predicts, 70 percent of those respondents who supported a redistribution policy to assist the poor at home also believed in supplying aid to poorer countries; 58 percent of those respondents who opposed redistribution also opposed economic aid (see table 4.7). Regarding the use of tough measures, respondents were asked about "banning the death penalty" at home and whether "it is necessary to use force to stop aggression; economic sanctions are not enough" when dealing with other countries. As table 4.8 shows, 65 percent of those respondents who were against the death penalty also disagreed with the use of force abroad; 69 percent who favored the death penalty also believed military force was necessary to stop foreign aggression. These findings support Lumsdaine's speculation

TABLE 4.7. The Relationship between Attitudes about Aiding the Poor at Home and Abroad, Two-by-Two Table, 1992 (in percentages)

		Aiding the Poor at Home (Columns)		
		Agree	Disagree	Total
Aiding the Poor Abroad (Rows)	Agree	70	42	54
	Disagree	30	58	46
	Total	100%	100%	100%
	N	276	349	625

Source: LOP panel data.
Note: Pearson chi-square = 50, DF = 1, $p < .01$.

that those who believe in toughness at home apply this value to policies aimed at other countries.[15]

However, if opinion leaders possess values that are operating in both domains, then different sets of these values appear to have co-alesced along a liberal-to-conservative continuum. In other words, I question whether we should conceive of opinion leaders' core values as discrete, free-floating elements. Notice, for instance, that respondents' attitudes toward "redistributing income from the wealthy to the poor" are associated with their views on "banning the death penalty." Indeed, 74 percent of those respondents who are against the death penalty favor redistribution; 71 percent of those who favor the death penalty are against redistribution (see table 4.9).

Apparently, the value toward assistance to the poor is inversely

TABLE 4.8.   The Relationship between Attitudes about Using Tough Measures at Home and Abroad, Two-by-Two Table, 1992 (in percentages)

| | | Banning the Death Penalty at Home (Columns) | | |
		Agree	Disagree	Total
Using Military Force Abroad (Rows)	Agree	35	69	57
	Disagree	65	31	43
	Total	100%	100%	100%
	N	210	404	614

Source: LOP panel data.
Note: Pearson chi-square = 64, DF = 1, $p < .01$.

TABLE 4.9.   The Relationship between Attitudes about Using Tough Measures at Home and Aiding the Poor at Home, Two-by-Two Table, 1992 (in percentages)

| | | Banning the Death Penalty at Home (Columns) | | |
		Agree	Disagree	Total
Aiding the Poor at Home (Rows)	Agree	74	29	44
	Disagree	26	71	56
	Total	100%	100%	100%
	N	212	408	620

Source: LOP panel data.
Note: Pearson chi-square = 112, DF = 1, $p < .01$.

related with the value toward the use of tough measures. Because these two issues are so closely associated, we can actually use respondents' domestic attitudes toward providing assistance to the poor to predict their foreign policy attitudes regarding the use of military force (table 4.10). Likewise, we can use respondents' attitudes toward the death penalty to predict their views on providing aid to poorer countries (table 4.11). And, as tables 4.12 to 4.15 show, all these question items are strongly associated with respondents' ideological orientations. We can see that liberals are much more likely than conservatives to support programs aimed at alleviating poverty, both at home and abroad (McClosky and Zaller 1984).[16] And the value of toughness, both at home and abroad, is associated with conservatism.[17]

The discrete values that Lumsdaine has highlighted as operating

TABLE 4.10.   The Relationship between Attitudes about Aiding the Poor at Home and Using Tough Measures Abroad, Two-by-Two Table, 1992 (in percentages)

		Aiding the Poor at Home (Columns)		
		Agree	Disagree	Total
Using Military Force Abroad (Rows)	Agree	40	71	57
	Disagree	60	29	43
	Total	100%	100%	100%
	N	279	356	635

Source: LOP panel data.
Note: Pearson chi-square = 64, DF = 1, $p < .01$.

TABLE 4.11.   The Relationship between Attitudes about Using Tough Measures at Home and Aiding the Poor Abroad, Two-by-Two Table, 1992 (in percentages)

		Banning the Death Penalty at Home (Columns)		
		Agree	Disagree	Total
Aiding the Poor Abroad (Rows)	Agree	74	44	54
	Disagree	26	56	46
	Total	100%	100%	100%
	N	205	400	605

Source: LOP panel data.
Note: Pearson chi-square = 49, DF = 1, $p < .01$.

TABLE 4.12. The Relationship between Ideological Orientations and Attitudes about Aiding the Poor at Home, 1992 (in percentages)

Response	Very Conservative	Somewhat Conservative	Moderate	Somewhat Liberal	Very Liberal
Agree	4	13	41	69	94
Disagree	96	87	59	31	6
Total	100	100	100	100	100
N	48	171	162	197	52

Source: LOP panel data.

Note: The Pearson chi-square = 203, DF = 4, $p < .01$. The few respondents who identified themselves as "far right" or "far left" are included in the "very conservative" and "very liberal" categories.

TABLE 4.13. The Relationship between Ideological Orientations and Attitudes about Aiding the Poor Abroad, 1992 (in percentages)

Response	Very Conservative	Somewhat Conservative	Moderate	Somewhat Liberal	Very Liberal
Agree	25	45	51	64	80
Disagree	75	55	49	36	20
Total	100	100	100	100	100
N	48	166	164	193	50

Source: LOP panel data.

Note: The Pearson chi-square = 43, DF = 4, $p < .01$. The percentages may not total one hundred due to rounding. The few respondents who identified themselves as "far right" or "far left" are included in the "very conservative" and "very liberal" categories.

TABLE 4.14. The Relationship between Ideological Orientations and Attitudes about Banning the Death Penalty, 1992 (in percentages)

Response	Very Conservative	Somewhat Conservative	Moderate	Somewhat Liberal	Very Liberal
Agree	2	8	25	58	83
Disagree	98	92	75	42	17
Total	100	100	100	100	100
N	47	165	154	192	52

Source: LOP panel data.

Note: The Pearson chi-square = 183, DF = 4, $p < .01$. The few respondents who identified themselves as "far right" or "far left" are included in the "very conservative" and "very liberal" categories.

TABLE 4.15.   The Relationship between Ideological Orientations and Attitudes about Using Tough Measures Abroad, 1992 (in percentages)

Response	Very Conservative	Somewhat Conservative	Moderate	Somewhat Liberal	Very Liberal
Agree	93	78	57	41	25
Disagree	7	22	43	59	75
Total	100	100	100	100	100
N	46	170	166	196	51

Source: LOP panel data.

Note: The Pearson chi-square = 95, DF = 4, $p < .01$. The few respondents who identified themselves as "far right" or "far left" are included in the "very conservative" and "very liberal" categories.

both in the international and domestic arenas appear to have coalesced along a left/right spectrum. Perhaps, then, the type of model implied by McClosky and Zaller (1984) needs to be considered. These authors argue that ideological groups tend to prioritize different values, such that modern liberals tend to be more supportive of the democratic values inherent in the American ethos while conservatives tend to be more supportive of the capitalistic values. To some extent, the values emphasized by each of these groups implies a strategy for how to treat other people. These strategies, in turn, may extend across domestic borders.

For instance, McClosky and Zaller note that liberals are more concerned about "social distress and material privation" at home and abroad. Using data collected from elite organizations with different ideological orientations in the 1970s, they found that 70 percent of liberal activists agreed that "if the world food shortage continues to get worse" then "we should greatly increase our effort to share our food with the hungry"; only 30 percent of the conservative activists chose this option (1984, 192–93). (Notice that these findings are similar to evidence presented in table 4.13.) They state that

> Our data . . . make it plain that, in their attitudes toward people who are outside their circles of personal acquaintance, conservatives are, as a group, less likely than liberals to favor action aimed at alleviating social distress. (McClosky and Zaller, 1984, 193–94)

In a similar approach, Alden and Schurmann note that left or liberal values in international affairs "have tended to be universalistic," while right or conservative values "have tended to be particularistic":

> The left has historically thought in terms of universal notions of justice—of natural rights and the common fate of mankind. . . .

The right, in contrast, has historically stressed the defense of the group—of one's family, community, or nation. (1990, 20–21)

It is possible, then, that the labels *conservative* and *liberal* reflect divergent sets of values and, accordingly, divergent beliefs about specific postures and policies, which are, in turn, loosely tied together into cognitive packages. Further, for leaders, these values and labels are meaningful both within and beyond the domestic arena.[18]

This does not necessarily mean, however, that the connections between foreign and domestic attitudes evident within elite belief systems comprise coherent, logically consistent philosophical systems. Indeed, it is often difficult to understand why some attitudes are grouped together under these ideological labels.

It is conceivable, for instance, that people derive their basic values through early socialization, and that these values provide a general orientation toward sociopolitical reality: for example, how to treat other people, what "goods" (security, human rights, etc.) deserve priority. The difference between opinion leaders and the mass public, then, could be that the former are more knowledgeable about the types of policies associated with the labels *liberalism* and *conservatism* and, hence, are more consistent in picking the labels most in line with their values. Alternatively, it is possible that the connections between the domains exhibited within elite beliefs may have been enhanced by "social learning."[19] Put differently, they participate in, and pay close attention to, the public debate; they incorporate widely held values and gain knowledge of "what goes with what" and why.[20]

To sum up, the evidence suggests that opinion leaders' general foreign policy postures and their domestic ideological orientations are both part of a common belief structure. A reasonable conjecture—which is consistent with, but cannot be confirmed by, the data here—is that respondents' general orientations toward both arenas are derived from common core values, and that different values have coalesced along a liberal-to-conservative continuum. If true, then opinion leaders' reactions to the end of the Cold War make sense. They adhered to basic values and strategies (perhaps "realist" or "neoliberal" in the language of international relations theory) about how to interact with other countries, and applied these values to new circumstances.

The Dimensionality of Elite Beliefs

One side issue raised by the evidence here concerns the dimensionality of opinion leaders' beliefs. As attitudes about domestic and foreign policy are closely interconnected, should elite belief systems be characterized as unidimensional, along a liberal-to-conservative continuum? This issue is important in light of past research, which characterizes leaders' foreign policy beliefs as structured according to principles or dimensions unique to that domain, and posits that their beliefs are bidimensional or even multidimensional (Wittkopf 1990, 1994; Holsti and Rosenau 1988, 1990, 1993; Holsti 1994; Chittick and Billingsley 1989).

The finding that opinion leaders' foreign policy postures are constrained by their domestic policy preferences does suggest that many attitudes in both domains fall along the liberal-to-conservative continuum. But by emphasizing that this dimension is important for understanding leaders' foreign policy beliefs, I do not mean to imply that it is the only one. Other dimensions may exist that are specific to domestic politics or to foreign policy. (For instance, attitudes about the Israeli-Palestinian conflict and attitudes about trade issues are not organized along the traditional ideological dimension.)

Indeed, the analysis provided here does not speak to the issue of how many dimensions characterize elite beliefs; it only stresses that the left-to-right spectrum is important across domains.

Let me try to illustrate the importance—not the singularity—of this dimension from a different angle. To start with, the individual questions that constitute the militant and cooperative internationalism scales (MI88, CI88) were used in a principal components factor analysis. Within this technique, the first unrotated factor is the single component that explains the largest amount of variance in the data (Kim and Mueller 1978). We can see in table 4.16 that the first component explained 40 percent of the variance in this instance.

Next, the individual questions that constitute the domestic policy preferences scale (DOM88) were used in a separate factor analysis. Each question had a high loading on the first unrotated factor—that factor that accounts for the greatest amount of variance (50 percent of the variance)—which suggests that all the questions share something in common (see table 4.17). It is certainly reasonable to assume that this first factor can be labeled *liberalism/conservatism*.

Then, respondents' factor scores from the foreign policy questions (the unrotated first factor) were correlated with their factor scores from the domestic questions (unrotated first factor). The correlation was high—at .67. When the same analysis was applied to the 1992 data, the correlation was .61 (see table 4.18). The implications of these findings are that (1) foreign policy and domestic attitudes have something in common, (2) the common feature may be called liberalism/conservatism, and (3) this dimension is an important principle within both domains.

TABLE 4.16.   Principal Components Factor Analysis, Unrotated, Foreign Policy Attitudes, 1988

Foreign Policy Questions	F1	F2
Militant Internationalism:		
There is nothing wrong with using the CIA to try to undermine hostile governments	0.67	−0.41
The conduct of American foreign affairs relies excessively on military advice	0.67	−0.41
Military aid programs will eventually draw the United States into unnecessary wars	0.57	−0.53
Military superiority of the United States (as an effective approach to world peace)	0.61	−0.43
Cooperative Internationalism:		
Fostering international cooperation to solve common problems, such as food, inflation, and energy (as a foreign policy goal)	0.62	0.27
Combating world hunger (as a foreign policy goal)	0.69	0.35
Helping to improve the standard of living in less-developed countries (as a foreign policy goal)	0.66	0.38
The United States should give economic aid to poorer countries even if it means higher prices at home	0.54	0.34
Protecting the global environment (as a foreign policy goal)	0.60	0.25
Worldwide arms control (as a foreign policy goal)	0.65	0.18
Strengthening the UN and other international organizations (as an effective approach to world peace)	0.66	0.01
Eigenvalues	4.4	1.4
Percentage of variance explained	40%	12%

Source: LOP panel data.

Note: Only factors with eigenvalues > 1 are included. The individual question items were rescaled to range from 0 to 1, and, in some cases the polarization was reversed. See table C.1.

TABLE 4.17.   Principal Components Factor Analysis, Unrotated, Domestic Policy Attitudes, 1988

Domestic Policy Questions	F1
Relaxing environmental regulation to stimulate economic growth	0.60
Barring homosexuals from teaching in public schools	0.73
Banning the death penalty	0.73
Redistributing income from the wealthy to the poor through taxation and subsidies	0.76
Permitting prayer in schools	0.71
Eigenvalues	2.5
Percentage of variance explained	50%

Source: LOP panel data.

Note: Only factors with eigenvalues > 1.0 are included. The individual question items were rescaled to range from 0 to 1, and, in some cases, the polarization was reversed. See table C.1.

Some may question the presumption that the common dimension linking the foreign policy and domestic domains can necessarily be characterized as liberalism/conservatism. A simple test puts these doubts to rest. Respondents were asked both in 1988 and 1992 how they would characterize themselves on an ideological scale ranging from far right to far left. Leaders' responses to this question are highly correlated with their factor scores from the domestic policy questions (first unrotated factor) and from the foreign policy questions (first unrotated factor) (see table 4.19).

To ensure that these results are not due to the selection of specific questions, the same analysis was applied to all fifty-five of the repeated foreign policy questions within the LOP panel study, and to the eight repeated domestic policy questions both for the 1988 wave and the 1992 wave (see the items marked with an asterisk in the 1992 LOP questionnaire shown in appendix D). The results were the same. The correlation between respondents' factor scores on the foreign policy questions

TABLE 4.18.   Correlations between First Unrotated Foreign Policy Component and First Unrotated Domestic Policy Component

Questions Used	Pearson Coefficient
MI/CI scales and domestic policy scale, 1988	0.67
MI/CI scales and domestic policy scale, 1992	0.61
All repeated foreign policy and domestic questions, 1988	0.74
All repeated foreign policy and domestic questions, 1992	0.75

Source: LOP panel data.

Note: For the wording of questions used in the MI/CI scales, see table C.1. For the wording of all repeated questions, see the marked (*) question items within the LOP 1992 questionnaire (appendix D).

TABLE 4.19.   Correlations between Respondents' Factor Scores and Their Ideological Self-Identification

	Pearson Coefficients	
Questions Used in Factor Analysis	1988	1992
Foreign policy postures [MI, CI]	0.68	0.54
Domestic policy beliefs [DOM]	0.73	0.78
All repeated foreign policy questions	0.73	0.68
All repeated domestic policy questions	0.73	0.77

Source: LOP panel data.

Note: The factor scores are from the first unrotated component in principal component factor analysis. For question items used in the MI/CI scales, see table C.1. For the wording of all repeated questions, see the marked (*) question items within the LOP questionnaire (appendix D).

(unrotated first factor) and their factor scores on the domestic questions (unrotated first factor) was .74 in 1988 and .75 in 1992 (see table 4.18). These factor scores were also highly correlated with respondents' ideological self-identification (see table 4.19).

Again, these findings suggest that the left/right spectrum is a useful predictor of leaders' foreign policy beliefs. This does not mean, however, that leaders' beliefs are unidimensional. The liberalism/conservatism dimension appears to dominate any other, but other dimensions are necessary to convey the complex relationships among a wide variety of political beliefs and preferences.

Conclusion

Recent research on the structure of leaders' foreign policy beliefs has tended to bifurcate these beliefs from the domestic policy domain. By breaking down this artificial barrier, we can account for the stability over time in leaders' foreign policy postures.[21]

I have demonstrated that "constraint" or "functional interdependence" existed between leaders' foreign policy postures and their domestic ideological orientations both before and after the end of the Cold War. The implication of this finding is that leaders' more general foreign policy postures and their domestic ideological orientations are both elements of the same belief system. (But by stating that liberalism/conservatism is an important dimension that organizes attitudes in both domains, I am not asserting that it is the *only* dimension.) The conjecture offered here is, first, that both types of beliefs are derived from the same core values and, second, that sets of values coalesce along the liberal-to-conservative continuum.

With this explanatory framework, the reaction of American opinion leaders to the end of the Cold War makes sense. The international arena had been transformed but the basic values that inform individuals' foreign policy decisions, and that tend to divide liberals from conservatives, remained constant. Leaders adhered to old orientations about how the United States should conduct itself in the world; they applied old values to new circumstances.

In the next chapter, I will discuss a possible implication of this analysis for the potential rebuilding of a foreign policy consensus. The evidence so far has demonstrated that leaders' basic foreign policy postures and their ideological orientations remained quite stable over time. It appears unlikely, then, that the gap dividing liberals and conservatives on foreign policy issues will have narrowed much with the end of the Cold War.

CHAPTER 5

Intellectual Baggage and the Prospects for Consensus

According to conventional wisdom, the American foreign policy establishment for two decades after the Second World War shared a broad vision, based primarily on anticommunism, about the goals the United States should pursue in the world (see Destler, Gelb, and Lake 1984; Wittkopf 1990).[1] The Vietnam War, so the story goes, shattered the Cold War consensus, and foreign policy again became the object of bitter contention and debate. Looking back from the mid-1980s, Destler, Gelb, and Lake describe the partisan bickering that resulted:

> the making of American foreign policy has been growing far more political—or more precisely, far more partisan and ideological. . . . [W]e Americans—politicians and experts alike—have been spending more time, energy and passion in fighting ourselves than we have in trying, as a nation, to understand and deal with a rapidly changing world. (1984, 13)

Now that the Cold War has ended, some observers of American politics have raised the question: can a new foreign policy consensus be forged?[2] Journalist Charles Krauthammer (1989/1990, 47), for instance, believes that

> In a post–Cold War world where communism is a spent force, there will be little to divide these adversaries. Left and Right internationalists will find common cause as they did in the early postwar years.

Likewise, Leslie Gelb (1992, A35), a columnist for the *New York Times,* states that

> It no longer makes any sense to speak of hawks and doves. Vietnam was Vietnam. The cold war was the cold war. The two old

battlegrounds—whether to send armed forces to fight "Soviet surro-
gates" in the third world and how much to spend on defense—have
largely vanished.[3]

And Jerry Sanders (1992, 367) perceives the "beginning of a new post–
Cold War bipartisanship" for the United States to take on a "leadership
role in promoting global democracy through a strategy of collective
engagement."

Certainly there are reasons to predict that ideological and partisan
divisiveness would diminish. Conceivably, the shock of the Soviet collapse, and the new international circumstances ushered in by that event,
could pry American opinion leaders out of their old, well-demarcated
political camps. And because changes within the international arena were
so profound, Americans have been forced to discard or recast political
debates—about such issues as nuclear policy or Soviet motivations—that
had dominated the foreign policy agenda for decades.

Of course, the loosening of old political allegiances and the recasting
of political debates need not lead to increased harmony (Hogan 1992).[4]
Tonelson (1993/1994), for instance, in an article titled "Beyond Left and
Right," articulates his perception that leadership coalitions within the
United States are undergoing a process of realignment, resulting in increased fragmentation (see also Weigel 1992). American conservatives,
he argues, have split into "three principal factions—conservative realists,
democratic crusaders, and conservative minimalists" (9). Meanwhile,
among some prominent liberals "an unmistakable new interventionism
has begun to take hold," resting on the "belief that the international
community is acquiring the right to intervene in the domestic affairs of
states when human rights are massively violated or order has broken
down" (13).

Tonelson dates the beginning of this realignment to the Persian Gulf
War (well before the second wave of the Leadership Opinion Project
[LOP] panel study). Before that event, the lines between liberal and
conservative political camps were well drawn:

> the more liberal someone was, the likelier it became that he would
> frown on using force to advance U.S. foreign policy goals rather
> than economic and diplomatic substitutes; to support acting multilat-
> erally rather than unilaterally; to give the Soviets the benefit of the
> doubt in international controversies; and to view Third World radi-
> cals as closet nationalists rather than communist stooges. The more
> conservative someone was, on the other hand, the likelier he was to
> take the opposite positions. (6)

But since the end of the Cold War, Tonelson asserts, the divisions between leadership groups have become much more fluid, confused, and
complicated:

> Not only are conservatives and liberals each divided into interven-
> tionists and non-interventionists on security issues, and nationalists
> and laissez-fairists on economics, but members of these new group-
> ings often disagree among themselves on foreign policy objectives.
> *In other words, conventional Cold War categories such as liberal and
> conservative . . . have lost their predictive power in the post–Cold
> War world.* (8; emphasis added)

In brief, Tonelson argues that during the post-Vietnam era, leadership
coalitions were split between conservative and liberal internationalists;
since the end of the Cold War, a multitude of new fissures have emerged,
breaking up these old coalitions.[5]

Judging by the LOP panel data, however, claims of major realign-
ments within leadership groups—regardless of whether those realign-
ments are expected to lead to increased harmony or fragmentation—are
greatly overstated. The evidence presented in earlier chapters demonstrated, first, that leaders' more general orientations toward the international arena remained stable and, second, that these orientations were
constrained by ideology over time. Such findings suggest the unlikeli-
hood that the divisions between ideological groups on many basic foreign policy issues have narrowed much following the end of the Cold
War, or that a transformation of old coalitions has taken place (at least
not by the spring of 1992).

Continued divisiveness between the left and the right on foreign
policy makes sense within the explanatory framework outlined in chapter 4. I have put forth the following two conjectures: leaders' basic
foreign policy postures are an expression of core values that inform their
orientations toward domestic policy as well; opposing values have become associated with different ideological labels. Hence, as leaders'
basic values were untouched by recent profound international events,
conservatives and liberals continue to embrace different strategies for
interacting with other countries.

The following discussion documents, in greater detail, the impact
that the end of the Cold War has had on ideological disagreements over
foreign policy through 1992. The first section demonstrates that fundamental divisions between conservatives and liberals persisted after the
Soviet collapse. The second section considers one source of this continuity, that is, whether respondents have drawn lessons from the end of the

Cold War, and then interpreted new national security issues, in a manner consistent with their past ideological orientations and values. The third section speculates, briefly, about what these findings, and the explanation proposed in chapter 4, may mean for the prospects of building a post–Cold War consensus.

The Persistence of Old Disagreements

Has the gap between ideological groups narrowed on basic issues regarding the use of military force or the importance of cooperating with other countries? Do we continue to find predictable differences between liberals and conservatives in the post–Cold War era?

The evidence suggests that, after the end of the Cold War, conservatives remained much more comfortable than liberals with the use of military instruments of power, and liberals remained more likely than conservatives to advocate cooperative ventures abroad.

On a few key issues, there has been a sea of change in opinion, and, in some cases, new agreement has emerged across ideological camps: in particular, both ideological groups reevaluated their views about the containment of communism and about the motivations of Russia. For instance, as shown in tables 5.1 to 5.4, conservatives and liberals, once polarized, landed on the same side of questions relating to the containment of communism by 1992.[6] When first asked about whether "there is considerable validity in the 'domino theory' that when one nation falls to communism, others nearby will soon follow a similar path," 75 percent of conservatives had agreed while 83 percent of liberals disagreed (table 5.1). But by 1992, the conservatives, responding to the collapse of communism in Eastern Europe and Russia, had changed their position: a majority of both ideological groups—62 percent of

TABLE 5.1. Ideological Groups' Differences on Attitudes about the Validity of the Domino Theory, 1988 (in percentages)

	Conservatives	Moderates	Liberals	Total
Agree	75	45	17	45
Disagree	25	55	83	55
Total	100%	100%	100%	100%
N	235	167	240	642

Source: LOP panel data.
Note: Pearson chi-square = 160, DF = 2, $p < .01$.

TABLE 5.2. Ideological Groups' Differences on Attitudes about the Validity of the Domino Theory, 1992 (in percentages)

	Conservatives	Moderates	Liberals	Total
Agree	38	30	10	25
Disagree	62	70	90	75
Total	100%	100%	100%	100%
N	215	166	249	630

Source: LOP panel data.
Note: Pearson chi-square = 53, DF = 2, $p < .01$.

TABLE 5.3. Ideological Groups' Differences on Attitudes toward the Use of Force to Stop Communist Spread, 1988 (in percentages)

	Conservatives	Moderates	Liberals	Total
Agree	61	27	10	33
Disagree	39	73	90	67
Total	100%	100%	100%	100%
N	232	165	235	632

Source: LOP panel data.
Note: Pearson chi-square = 144, DF = 2, $p < .01$.

TABLE 5.4. Ideological Groups' Differences on Attitudes toward the Use of Force to Stop Communist Spread, 1992 (in percentages)

	Conservatives	Moderates	Liberals	Total
Agree	39	28	10	24
Disagree	61	73	90	76
Total	100%	100%	100%	100%
N	212	160	247	619

Source: LOP panel data.
Note: Percentages may not total one hundred exactly due to rounding. Pearson chi-square = 52, DF = 2, $p < .01$.

conservatives and 90 percent of liberals—now disputed the theory (table 5.2).

Likewise, when asked in 1988 whether the United States "should take all steps including the use of force to prevent the spread of communism," 61 percent of conservatives had agreed whereas 90 percent of liberals disagreed (table 5.3): again, by 1992, many conservatives had changed their views and a majority of both ideological groups disagreed with this statement (table 5.4).

Liberals and conservatives alike reassessed their views about the expansionist tendencies of the Soviet Union-Russia between 1988 and 1992 in response to changes within that country. When asked in 1988 whether "The Soviet Union is generally expansionist rather than defensive in its foreign policy goals," 89 percent of conservatives agreed along with 55 percent of liberals (table 5.5). When asked in 1992 to predict whether "Once their economy stabilizes, Russia will become an expansionist power," 75 percent of conservatives and 94 percent of liberals disagreed (table 5.6).

TABLE 5.5.   Ideological Groups' Differences on Whether the Soviet Union Is Expansionist, 1988 (in percentages)

	Conservatives	Moderates	Liberals	Total
Agree	89	77	55	73
Disagree	11	23	45	27
Total	100%	100%	100%	100%
N	232	164	239	635

Source: LOP panel data.
Note: Pearson chi-square = 71, DF = 2, $p < .01$.

TABLE 5.6.   Ideological Groups' Differences on Whether Russia Has Expansionist Tendencies, 1992 (in percentages)

	Conservatives	Moderates	Liberals	Total
Agree	25	20	6	16
Disagree	75	80	94	84
Total	100%	100%	100%	100%
N	199	149	229	577

Source: LOP panel data.
Note: Pearson chi-square = 29, DF = 2, $p < .01$.

The implications of these changes should not be understated: the abandonment of containment policy marks a major turning point in the history of American foreign policy. But, as further investigation will show, ideological groups remained polarized, despite the end of the Cold War, over fundamental approaches about how best to interact with other countries.

More specifically, table 5.7 presents the size of the gap in conservatives' and liberals' mean scores on scales measuring their stances toward militant and cooperative internationalism (MI, CI) both in 1988 and 1992. (Remember that each of these scales has a range of zero to one. See appendix C for details about how the MI and CI scales were constructed.) When considering respondents' general postures toward cooperative internationalism, we see an absolute difference of .25 between the mean scores of the two groups in 1988, which narrowed slightly to .19 by 1992. We see the same pattern for their general stances toward militant internationalism: the difference between the means of conservatives and liberals was .36 in 1988, and it narrowed to .26 by 1992. Although smaller by 1992, the gap between conservatives and liberals remained quite substantial, as well as statistically significant, for each posture.

A much simpler illustration of the continued disagreement between conservatives and liberals over issues related to militant and cooperative internationalism can be achieved by considering individual question items. Tables 5.8 to 5.15, for example, present liberals' and conservatives' stances over time on various questions about the use of military instruments of power.[7] We can see that in each instance the two ideological groups were on opposite sides of the issue in 1988 and remained so in 1992.

For example, 71 percent of conservatives agreed in 1988 that "There is nothing wrong with using the C.I.A. to try to undermine hostile govern-

TABLE 5.7. The Gap between Conservatives' and Liberals' Stances on MI and CI, Difference of Means, 1988 and 1992

Posture	Mean Scores in 1988			Mean Scores in 1992		
	Consrv.	Liberal	Gap	Consrv.	Liberal	Gap
MI	0.32	0.68	0.36	0.34	0.60	0.26
CI	0.59	0.84	0.25	0.60	0.79	0.19
	$N = 237$	$N = 242$		$N = 222$	$N = 252$	

Source: LOP panel data.

Note: MI refers to militant internationalism, CI to cooperative internationalism. See table C.1 for the question items used to create these scales.

ments": 84 percent of liberals disagreed (table 5.8). That split was still quite apparent by 1992: 64 percent of conservatives agreed and 74 percent of liberals disagreed (table 5.9). Likewise, when respondents were asked in 1988 whether the "military superiority of the United States" was an effective approach to "world peace," 93 percent of conservatives thought it was "very effective" or "moderately effective" whereas 54 percent of liberals thought it was only "slightly effective" or "not at all effective" (table 5.14); again, the polarization between these ideological groups did not change much by 1992 (table 5.15). And the same pattern is apparent in the ideological groups' responses over time to other military-related statements (tables 5.10 to 5.13).

Conservatives and liberals also continued to disagree on most issues regarding cooperative activities with other countries (tables 5.16 to 5.19). When asked whether "The United States should give economic aid to poorer countries even if it means higher prices at home," 84 percent of liberals agreed in 1988, whereas 60 percent of conservatives disagreed (table 5.16). Their positions remained polarized—although

TABLE 5.8.   Ideological Groups' Differences on Attitudes toward the Use of Covert Activities by the CIA, 1988 (in percentages)

	Conservatives	Moderates	Liberals	Total
Agree	71	43	16	43
Disagree	29	57	84	57
Total	100%	100%	100%	100%
N	231	166	236	633

Source: LOP panel data.
Note: Pearson chi-square = 148, DF = 2, $p < .01$.

TABLE 5.9.   Ideological Groups' Differences on Attitudes toward the Use of Covert Activities by the CIA, 1992 (in percentages)

	Conservatives	Moderates	Liberals	Total
Agree	64	52	26	45
Disagree	36	48	74	55
Total	100%	100%	100%	100%
N	214	166	249	629

Source: LOP panel data.
Note: Pearson chi-square = 70, DF = 2, $p < .01$.

TABLE 5.10. Ideological Groups' Differences on Attitudes about Whether U.S. Foreign Policy Relies Too Much on Military Advice, 1988 (in percentages)

	Conservatives	Moderates	Liberals	Total
Agree	38	65	87	64
Disagree	62	35	13	36
Total	100%	100%	100%	100%
N	230	165	239	634

Source: LOP panel data.
Note: Pearson chi-square = 123, DF = 2, $p < .01$.

TABLE 5.11. Ideological Groups' Differences on Attitudes about Whether U.S. Foreign Policy Relies Too Much on Military Advice, 1992 (in percentages)

	Conservatives	Moderates	Liberals	Total
Agree	24	43	68	46
Disagree	76	57	32	54
Total	100%	100%	100%	100%
N	209	164	244	617

Source: LOP panel data.
Note: Pearson chi-square = 86, DF = 2, $p < .01$.

TABLE 5.12. Ideological Groups' Differences on Attitudes about Whether Military Aid Draws the United States into Unnecessary Wars, 1988 (in percentages)

	Conservatives	Moderates	Liberals	Total
Agree	24	46	70	47
Disagree	76	54	30	53
Total	100%	100%	100%	100%
N	233	165	235	633

Source: LOP panel data.
Note: Pearson chi-square = 100, DF = 2, $p < .01$.

TABLE 5.13. Ideological Groups' Differences on Attitudes about Whether Military Aid Draws the United States into Unnecessary Wars, 1992 (in percentages)

	Conservatives	Moderates	Liberals	Total
Agree	26	41	60	43
Disagree	74	59	40	57
Total	100%	100%	100%	100%
N	210	166	241	617

Source: LOP panel data.
Note: Pearson chi-square = 52, DF = 2, $p < .01$.

TABLE 5.14. Ideological Groups' Differences on Attitudes about Whether U.S. Military Superiority Is an Effective Approach to World Peace, 1988 (in percentages)

	Conservatives	Moderates	Liberals	Total
Effective	93	70	46	69
Not Effective	7	30	54	31
Total	100%	100%	100%	100%
N	235	169	235	639

Source: LOP panel data.
Note: The "effective" category includes the "very" and "moderately" response options. The "not effective" category includes "slightly" or "not at all" response options. Pearson chi-square = 121, DF = 2, $p < .01$.

TABLE 5.15. Ideological Groups' Differences on Attitudes about Whether U.S. Military Superiority Is an Effective Approach to World Peace, 1992 (in percentages)

	Conservatives	Moderates	Liberals	Total
Effective	87	79	49	70
Not Effective	13	21	51	30
Total	100%	100%	100%	100%
N	217	163	249	629

Source: LOP panel data.
Note: The "effective" category includes the "very" and "moderately" response options. The "not effective" category includes "slightly" or "not at all" response options. Pearson chi-square = 85, DF = 2, $p < .01$.

slightly less so—in 1992: by then 67 percent of liberals agreed and 59 percent of conservatives disagreed (table 5.17).

Likewise, when asked about the importance of "Combatting world hunger," conservatives and liberals were again on different sides of the issue in both panel waves. In 1988, 78 percent of liberals regarded this goal as "very important" whereas 55 percent of conservatives thought it was only "somewhat important" (table 5.18); by 1992, fewer liberals thought it was "very important" than before—63 percent—but still a strong majority, whereas 57 percent of conservatives still thought it was only "somewhat important" (table 5.19).[8]

On other questions that tap cooperative internationalism, the differences between conservatives and liberals have remained profound as well. A majority of respondents from both sides of the ideological divide agreed that "Fostering international cooperation to solve common problems, such as food, inflation, and energy" was "very important" in 1988; there were similar findings in 1992 (tables 5.20 and 5.21). Still, the difference in the amount of support between the groups was profound:

TABLE 5.16. Ideological Groups' Differences on Attitudes about Aiding Poorer Countries, 1988 (in percentages)

	Conservatives	Moderates	Liberals	Total
Agree	40	61	84	62
Disagree	60	39	16	38
Total	100%	100%	100%	100%
N	232	160	234	626

Source: LOP panel data.
Note: Pearson chi-square = 96, DF = 2, $p < .01$.

TABLE 5.17. Ideological Groups' Differences on Attitudes about Aiding Poorer Countries, 1992 (in percentages)

	Conservatives	Moderates	Liberals	Total
Agree	41	51	67	54
Disagree	59	49	33	46
Total	100%	100%	100%	100%
N	214	164	243	621

Source: LOP panel data.
Note: Pearson chi-square = 33, DF = 2, $p < .01$.

TABLE 5.18. Ideological Groups' Differences on Attitudes about the Importance of Combating World Hunger, 1988 (in percentages)

	Conservatives	Moderates	Liberals	Total
Very	34	62	78	58
Somewhat	55	37	20	37
Not	11	1	1	5
Total	100%	100%	100%	100%
N	231	167	237	635

Source: LOP panel data.
Note: The percentages may not total one hundred exactly due to rounding. Pearson chi-square = 108, DF = 4, $p < .01$.

TABLE 5.19. Ideological Groups' Differences on Attitudes about the Importance of Combating World Hunger, 1992 (in percentages)

	Conservatives	Moderates	Liberals	Total
Very	27	49	63	47
Somewhat	57	46	35	45
Not	15	5	2	7
Total	100%	100%	100%	100%
N	215	164	252	631

Source: LOP panel data.
Note: The percentages may not total one hundred exactly due to rounding. Pearson chi-square = 76, DF = 4, $p < .01$.

TABLE 5.20. Ideological Groups' Differences on Attitudes about the Importance of Fostering International Cooperation, 1988 (in percentages)

	Conservatives	Moderates	Liberals	Total
Very	52	80	87	72
Somewhat	45	20	13	26
Not	3	1	0	1
Total	100%	100%	100%	100%
N	235	167	238	640

Source: LOP panel data.
Note: The percentages may not total one hundred exactly due to rounding. Pearson chi-square = 81, DF = 4, $p < .01$.

TABLE 5.21.   Ideological Groups' Differences on Attitudes about the Importance of Fostering International Cooperation, 1992 (in percentages)

	Conservatives	Moderates	Liberals	Total
Very	47	69	78	65
Somewhat	48	30	21	32
Not	5	2	1	3
Total	100%	100%	100%	100%
N	220	166	250	636

Source: LOP panel data.

Note: The percentages may not total one hundred exactly due to rounding. Pearson chi-square = 53, DF = 4, $p < .01$.

52 percent of conservatives and 87 percent of liberals chose the "very important" response option in 1988, a gap of thirty-five percentage points; 47 percent of conservatives and 78 percent of liberals chose that option in 1992, a gap of thirty-one percentage points. A similar pattern is seen on questions about the importance of "protecting the international environment" and "worldwide arms control" as U.S. foreign policy goals. In each case, a substantial proportion of both ideological groups believed that these goals were "very important" both in 1988 and 1992; still, there was a large gap between the percentage of liberals and the percentage of conservatives who chose this option.[9]

On a few questions that tap cooperative internationalism, we do find that the ideological groups have changed their views. Specifically, there was movement within the liberal camp on the question of whether "Helping to improve the standard of living in less developed countries" is a "very important" foreign policy goal: they dropped from 73 percent in 1988 to 44 percent in 1992 (the comparable percentages for conservatives are 28 percent in 1988 and 18 percent in 1992). Even so, a large difference remained between the ideological groups: a gap of twenty-six percentage points in 1992.

And both ideological groups changed their views on the effectiveness of the United Nations. When asked about "Strengthening the UN and other international organizations" as "an approach to world peace," only 26 percent of conservatives, compared to 68 percent of liberals, thought that this was either an "effective" or "moderately effective" tactic in 1988. However, 60 percent of conservatives and 85 percent of liberals chose those response options in 1992, probably in reaction to the role the United Nations played during the Persian Gulf War.[10]

Altogether, the evidence suggests that conservatives and liberals have continued to embrace different strategies for approaching foreign affairs. Whether concerning the use of military power or cooperative efforts to help other countries, the differences between the groups remained wide over time, and, in most cases, a majority of conservatives and liberals still sat on opposite sides of the issue by 1992. Divisions over military-related issues remained especially clear-cut.

Old Ideological Orientations and New Circumstances

Conservatives and liberals may have interpreted the lessons of the end of the Cold War in a manner that verified their own particular values and strategies toward foreign affairs. As Deudney and Ikenberry (1992, 123) note,

> The emerging debate over why the Cold War ended is of more than historical interest: At stake is the vindication and legitimation of an entire world view and foreign policy orientation.

After the revolutions in Eastern Europe, conservatives began to claim credit for the collapse of communism (Kinsley 1989, 4). The enormous U.S. military buildup in the early 1980s, they reasoned, had precipitated Soviet capitulation in the Cold War; they believed that the Reagan strategy of "peace through strength" had worked. Spokespeople on the liberal left, in contrast, tended to attribute the Soviet collapse to weaknesses internal to that country, not to the success of military confrontation by the United States. Further, they highlighted the high costs such a strategy had had for the United States (Kennedy 1987). Richard Barnet (1992, 126), for example, articulates this view:

> The costs of the prolonged political-military struggle that Lippmann called the Cold War can be counted not only in the neglect and deterioration of domestic institutions but also in the loss of American capacity to exercise constructive influence abroad. The world's only global superpower lacks the material resources to maintain a competitive industrial base, the infrastructure on which a strong economy depends, or even the necessities, much less the amenities, of a good society.

Data from the LOP panel reveal an association between leaders' 1988 ideological orientations and their causal interpretations, as expressed in 1992, about the "reasons . . . the Soviet leadership initiated reforms at home and permitted the collapse of the Soviet empire in Eastern Europe" (table 5.22).[11] Almost everybody, regardless of their past beliefs, agreed that the economic crisis within the Soviet Union was the primary cause of the political reform there. But people who identi- fied themselves as conservatives in 1988 were more likely than liberals to believe that "the U.S. military build-up during the Reagan era" forced the Soviets to change ($r = .41$); and conservatives were less likely than liberals to rate "a new generation of Soviet leaders with different foreign policy goals" as an important causal factor ($r = -.28$).

Respondents' past ideological stances are also associated with their perceptions about the costs of the Cold War for the United States. They were asked in 1992 whether "The United States overextended itself in the fight against communism."[12] Of those respondents who had identified themselves as liberals in 1988, 79 percent agreed with this statement; of those who had identified themselves as conservatives, 63 percent dis- agreed (table 5.23).

These data suggest that respondents' past values and beliefs con- cerning the use of military force influenced what lessons they drew from the end of the Cold War. Conservatives, who as a group had tended to advocate the assertive use of military force, were more likely to believe

TABLE 5.22.   The Relationship between Leaders' Past Beliefs and Their Causal Interpretations about Changes in Soviet Behavior, Pearson Coefficients, 1988 and 1992

Reasons the Soviet Leadership Initiated Reform 1992 (items ranked 1 to 5)	Past Beliefs, 1988			
	Ideological Orientations		Militant Internationalism	
	R	N	R	N
The economic crisis in the Soviet Union	−0.09	652	−0.10	652
The U.S. military buildup during the Reagan era	0.41	623	0.51	623
A new generation of Soviet lead- ers with different foreign policy goals	−0.28	642	−0.34	642
The Western alliance's sustained commitment to contain communism	0.13	620	0.22	620
The failure of communism to pro- vide basic political freedoms	−0.17	628	−0.27	628

Source: LOP panel data.

Note: The correlations are pairwise.

in 1992 that this strategy had helped to end the Cold War; liberals, who as a group had tended to contest the use of military force, were likely to place more credence on factors internal to the Soviet Union. And conservatives were less likely to believe that the Cold War had hurt—or overextended—the United States; whereas liberals were more likely to perceive the United States as exhausted and weakened from the diversion of resources used to confront the Soviet Union.

Not surprisingly, then, the gap between how conservatives and liberals interpreted new security issues was also large. Table 5.24 compares how people who had identified themselves as conservatives or as liberals in 1988 responded to six military policy items "for a post–Cold War era" asked in 1992. The first four question items in the table are about whether the United States "needs to keep ahead of Russia in strategic nuclear weapons," whether the United States "can now dismantle most of its strategic nuclear weapons," whether the United States "needs to develop SDI to protect against accidental and limited nuclear attacks," and whether the United States "should close most of its foreign military bases." In each instance, a majority of those respondents who had identified themselves as conservatives in 1988 took the promilitary stance in 1992, while a majority of those respondents who had identified themselves as liberals took the antimilitary stance.

On the two final policy issues—about maintaining "high levels of defense spending" and about limiting the "CIA's activities . . . to intelligence gathering"—a majority of each group sat on the same side of the issue. But the gap between the groups was still large: of those who had identified themselves as conservatives in 1988, 55 percent disagreed with maintaining high levels of defense spending in 1992, compared with 93

TABLE 5.23.   The Relationship between Leaders' Past Ideological Orientations and Their 1992 Attitudes about the Costs of the Cold War (in percentages)

		Time 1 Ideological Orientations, 1988 (Columns)			Total
		Conservatives	Moderates	Liberals	
Time 2					
U.S. Overextended due to	Agree	37	62	79	59
Cold War 1992	Disagree	63	38	21	41
(Rows)	Total	100%	100%	100%	100%
	N	230	163	237	630

Source: LOP panel data.
Note: Pearson chi-square = 89, DF = 2, $p < .01$.

percent of those respondents who had identified themselves as liberals—a gap of thirty-eight percentage points. And 84 percent of those who had identified themselves as liberals agreed that the CIA's activities needed to be limited, compared with 52 percent of those who had identified themselves as conservatives—a gap of thirty-two percentage points.

Finally, the differences between liberals and conservatives remained profound, and in the predictable direction, on more general statements about the types of strategies the United States should pursue in world affairs (see table 5.25). In 1992, conservatives were still much more likely than liberals to believe that only military force—not other tactics such as diplomacy or economic sanctions—can counter aggression, to legitimize the unilateral use of force, to tolerate U.S. support of dictators, and to believe that the United States must keep a vigilant guard against potential aggressors. They were less likely to consider human rights to be a very important foreign policy goal.

We have seen here that conservatives and liberals continued to approach issues related to militant and cooperative internationalism

TABLE 5.24.   The Relationship between Leaders' Past Ideological Orientations and Their 1992 Attitudes about Post–Cold War Issues (percentage agreeing, part 1)

Views of U.S. Foreign Policy in the Post–Cold War Era, 1992	Ideological Orientations, 1988		
	Conservatives	Moderates	Liberals
The United States needs to keep ahead of Russia in strategic nuclear weapons	79	66	40
The United States can now dismantle most of its strategic nuclear weapons	36	56	77
The United States needs to develop SDI to protect against accidental and limited nuclear attacks	81	53	19
The United States should close most of its foreign military bases	43	48	69
The CIA's activities should be limited to intelligence gathering	52	71	84
Because the future is uncertain the United States needs to maintain high levels of defense spending	45	22	7

Source: LOP panel data.

TABLE 5.25. The Relationship between Leaders' Past Ideological Orientations and Their 1992 Attitudes about Post–Cold War Issues (percentage agreeing, part 2)

Views of U.S. Foreign Policy in the Post–Cold War Era, 1992	Ideological Orientations, 1988		
	Conservatives	Moderates	Liberals
It is necessary to use military force to stop aggression; economic sanctions are not enough	78	59	37
The collapse of the Soviet Union does not mean that the United States can let down its guard; there will always be powerful, aggressive nations in the world	94	75	57
The United States may have to support some dictators because they are friendly toward us	59	41	22
The highest priority of American foreign policy should be the enhancement of our national power	42	38	14
There is nothing wrong with the United States unilaterally using military force abroad	46	30	12
Promoting and defending human rights in other countries (as a U.S. foreign policy goal)*	18	41	49

Source: LOP panel data.
Note: *Percentage who believe this goal is "very important."

much as they did before the end of the Cold War. In addition, respondents appear to have interpreted new events (such as the Soviet collapse) and post–Cold War national security issues in a manner consistent with past beliefs, ideological orientations, and values.

Is Consensus Possible?

As I noted earlier, the finding that conservatives and liberals continued to disagree on many basic foreign policy issues is consistent with my earlier explanatory framework: that is, individuals within these different ideological groups embrace different values and strategies for how best to interact with other countries, and they adhered to these values despite profound changes in the international arena.

But if this explanation is correct, how then was a foreign policy consensus ever possible? Certainly American leaders did not share common core values in the two decades between the 1940s and the 1960s: politics may have stopped at the water's edge, but it did not disappear all together. Liberals and conservatives fought over domestic politics during those years. And if core values inform preferences in both the domestic and foreign policy arenas, then why was one sphere fraught with partisan conflict while the other possessed some measure of bipartisan unity? (Wildavsky 1966, 1991 ch. 3)

Full treatment of this question is beyond the scope of this study. However, past scholarship does offer some initial clues. One explanation is that leaders who embraced divergent core values made a bargain that allowed them to agree on the goals of foreign policy for a time. Hughes (1980, 50), for instance, believes that the "United States has in fact two cultures of foreign policy—the security culture and the equity culture"—categories that can be easily translated into the terms of conservatism and liberalism. He (1980, 52) writes that

> The conventional wisdom is that there was a foreign policy consensus in the United States for 20 years after World War II that broke up over Vietnam. . . . It is popularly supposed to have been built around containment, and the assumption is that most Americans were somehow in basic agreement about shared foreign policy goals.
>
> In fact, this was never the case. Instead, during those halcyon years there was a workable dissensus that has now, for a variety of reasons, become unworkable.

During the years between the Second World War and the Vietnam War, adherents of these two cultures made "a tacit bargain":

> The security culture and the equity culture were there all along, but the earlier dissensus was positive because the two cultures resolved their doubts in favor of the coalition and thereby allowed foreign policy to function. (1980, 53)

Following a similar logic, Alden and Schurmann (1990, 22) make a useful distinction between a policy consensus and a value consensus.

> A value consensus is one in which all or most decision-makers and all or most of the public share the values on which a policy is based. . . . A policy consensus, on the other hand, is one in which opponents agree on a particular policy as a workable compromise among competing values.

The Cold War consensus, they argue, was "primarily a policy consensus—a compromise between left and right values."

> Containment promised a vigilant stance toward the Soviets, and later the Chinese, thus accommodating the concerns of the right, and it promised the construction of a just and prosperous global order within the "free world," thus speaking to the liberal-left agenda. The various elements which comprised the containment policy were proffered by competing ideological currents—world order and the construction of international organizations coming from the liberal/left wing; anti-communism and vigilant national security from the right. Containment made these visions operational by integrating competing values and weaving them into an executive-led strategy for American foreign policy which was relatively insulated from the buffeting of ideological currents.

The Vietnam War undermined that policy consensus, and reopened competitive ideological struggles over the direction of American foreign policy.

In each of these explanations, the core values embraced by Americans—and the political divisions that such divergent values engendered—maintained a continuity over time. However, in some political circumstances, these opposing camps could agree on policy, albeit for different reasons.

With this qualification in mind, let us rephrase the more current question: has the end of the Cold War created new circumstances that would again permit a "workable dissensus" on foreign policy? Any response to this question can only be speculative. That said, it is clear that the demise of the bipolar superpower rivalry has permitted a new fluidity within the international arena. Issues that a few years ago would have been unthinkable have been thrust onto the agenda. And as novel situations arise, they may create value conflicts within each ideological camp that can possibly lead to short-term bargains. For instance, the post–Cold War situations in Bosnia-Hercegovina or Somalia highlight human rights and the alleviation of distress as reasons for military action, values that speak to liberals, normally loath to turn to arms.[13] Under these conditions, dovish liberals might be provoked to join hawkish conservatives. Indeed, some have seen Americans' reactions toward Bosnia "as the beginning of a durable post–Cold War coalition of centrist internationalists." But, as commentator Robert Wright (1993, 22) noted in the *New Republic*, "this label conceals some differences." "Cold war doves," he continued, may tend to support intervention for humanitarian reasons, while cold war hawks (in their heart of hearts) are driven more by law-and-order concerns—the fear of spreading chaos.[14]

In other words, the fluidity of post–Cold War circumstances may allow new situations to arise that speak to core values—albeit different values—of both conservatives and liberals. At the same time, however, the evidence suggests that the differences between these groups remain deep. Barring a threatening crisis, a workable dissensus would probably have to be forged on a case-by-case basis (Chace 1978).

Conclusion

Between 1988 and 1992, both liberals and conservatives reevaluated their views about the motivations of Russia, and conservatives, in particular, discarded the containment of communism as the preeminent policy. But still, deep divisions persisted between these ideological groups. They continued to disagree about how best to interact with other countries.

Continued divisiveness between ideological groups makes sense within the interpretation provided in chapter 4. I suggested that American leaders' orientations toward politics—whether in the domestic or international arena—may be derived from their core values, and that divergent values, in turn, have become associated with the ideological labels *conservative* and *liberal*. As leaders' values and ideological identifications remained constant despite changes in the international arena, so did their basic foreign policy postures; hence, the traditional political divisions between American leaders were not much affected by the end of the Cold War.

CHAPTER 6

Conclusion

The reaction of American leaders to the end of the Cold War can be described as a mixture of attitude continuity and change. On the one hand, the Leadership Opinion Project (LOP) respondents adjusted their beliefs to account for the Soviet collapse. They revised their perceptions about the nature and intentions of Russia, abandoned containment policy as an important guidepost of American foreign policy, and reevaluated some national security issues, such as defense spending. These changes in leaders' beliefs should make an enormous difference in the conduct of American foreign policy.[1]

On the other hand, American leaders adhered to old predispositions about how the United States should interact with other countries. The evidence demonstrates an impressive continuity over time in attitudes about the projection of military power abroad and about involvement in cooperative efforts to help other nations. Leaders had embraced different postures or strategies about how best to interact with other countries before the end of the Cold War, and upheavals within the international system did not alter their convictions, at least not by 1992.

These findings provide some important clues about the structure and sources of elite foreign policy beliefs: the external international environment changed profoundly, and yet the LOP respondents' basic foreign policy postures remained stable. The reason for this continuity in foreign policy postures, I have argued, is that they were bound together with, and constrained by, domestic ideological orientations. Indeed, ideology has proved to be a powerful predictor of militant and cooperative internationalism both before and after the end of the Cold War. Overall, the evidence suggests that ideology matters: leaders' ideological predispositions, and perhaps their core values, are important factors in how they perceive and approach international politics.

This finding, in turn, implies that foreign and domestic policy attitudes are more interconnected within elite belief systems than is suggested by recent literature. Scholars have tended to treat these domains as two relatively independent, albeit overlapping, belief systems. But the evidence suggests that "constraint" or "functional interdependence" exists between domestic and foreign policy attitudes over time, and that the separation of these domains is artificial. That is not to say, however, that elite belief structure is unidimensional, only that the liberal-to-conservative dimension is an important predictor of both domestic and foreign policy opinions.

While this study has demonstrated the interconnection between domestic and foreign policy attitudes within elite belief systems, the nature of this connection requires some further investigation. A reasonable explanation for the across-domain constraint over time is that foreign policy and domestic beliefs are both derived from common core values. I have proposed that different values have become associated with the ideological labels *conservative* and *liberal,* and that leaders apply these values both within and beyond the domestic borders. As leaders' core values did not change when the Soviet Union collapsed, their basic beliefs about how best to treat other countries also remained stable. This explanation is consistent with the evidence, but it cannot be tested adequately with the LOP panel data.

Direct measures of leaders' core values along with questions about domestic and foreign policy issues are needed to investigate this model more fully. To build on the analysis here, a future research project could use the survey format or in-depth interviews to determine with more precision the specific values that distinguish liberals from conservatives, to uncover which values tend to coalesce together under these different ideological labels, and to identify the values that apply across domains.

Additional information about the relationship between leaders' values, their ideological orientations, and their foreign policy beliefs might allow us to understand better the conditions that permit broad-based agreement on foreign policy. I have demonstrated that the gap between ideological groups on many basic foreign policy issues remained substantial despite the end of the Cold War. Conservatives were much more likely than liberals, over time, to approve of the use of military instruments of power, and liberals remained much more likely than conservatives, over time, to believe that the United States should aid other countries and participate in joint ventures to solve international problems. This finding makes sense within the explanatory framework offered here: ideological groups have brought old values to new circumstances. But with more knowledge about the specific values associated with ideological groups, it may be possible to predict how members of those groups would react to various environmental circumstances: in other words, to determine what types of circumstances are conducive to "tacit bargains" between ideological groups and what circumstances are likely to create polarization.

Another important question left for future study is how the belief structure of U.S. leaders compares with that of leadership groups from other countries. This study has shown that the labels *conservatism* and *liberalism* are quite predictive of American leaders' domestic and foreign policy beliefs and has suggested that the differences between these ideological groups are rooted in basic values. It would be informative to extend the analysis to other countries and compare both the underlying values and the organizing dimensions that structure beliefs across different leadership groups.

While some issues raised here call for further investigation, one finding can be stated unambiguously: leaders' domestic and foreign policy beliefs are intertwined. Leaders' basic strategies for how to treat other peoples, and even their perceptions about the reasons why the Cold War ended, are grounded in their ideological convictions. If future studies about the structure and sources of leaders' foreign policy beliefs divorce such attitudes from domestic beliefs, they will be leaving out an important piece of the puzzle.

Appendixes

Construction of the LOP Panel Study

The purpose of this appendix is to detail the procedures used to create the Leadership Opinion Project (LOP) data set and to assess its quality.[1]

The LOP study was constructed in an unusual manner due to extraordinary historical circumstances. The end of the Cold War created an unprecedented opportunity to study the processes of change in Americans' foreign policy beliefs. Without doubt, the most appropriate research design to investigate this subject matter—that is, change in beliefs over time—is a panel study. But no researcher was prescient enough to begin the first wave of a panel study before the sudden onset of the cumulative events that ended the Cold War era. Because I wanted to make inferences based on panel data, my only available option was to extend an already existing cross-sectional survey.[2] Accordingly, I created the LOP data set, with the cooperation of Ole Holsti and James Rosenau, by adding a second wave onto their 1988 Foreign Policy Leadership Project (FPLP) survey.[3]

The following discussion consists of three sections. I begin with a description of Holsti and Rosenau's sampling procedures. Following that, I detail my own procedures for adding a second wave. Finally, I demonstrate that these latter procedures did not skew the results of the panel.

Sampling Procedures in 1988

The 1988 FPLP cross-sectional survey laid the foundation for the LOP panel study. Hence, to assess the quality of the LOP panel, we must first consider the sampling procedures used by Holsti and Rosenau.

They operated under two assumptions. First, they did not attempt to "faithfully and precisely" replicate "society's leadership structure" (Holsti 1990a, 4). Holsti and Rosenau considered such an "elusive ideal sample" unattainable.

This assumption is by no means unusual. Indeed, it is difficult to understand how they could have drawn a representative elite sample even if they had wanted to. Nobody has attempted it, and for good reason. The question of how many and which Americans constitute the political elite is highly disputed and largely definitional. Some researchers might focus on highly placed public officials, others on corporate leaders, and still others on a broad spectrum of "opinion makers."[4] As McClosky and Zaller (1984, 14) note,

> Unlike the general population, whose members can be randomly drawn from a known universe and whose characteristics can, if necessary, be checked against census data, there is no known, agreed-upon universe of elite members from which a genuine random sample can be drawn.

Therefore, the 1988 FPLP survey, just like all other elite studies, cannot "describe the foreign policy views of leaders in the aggregate, in a manner comparable to a public opinion poll" (Holsti 1990a, 4). That limitation, however, does not undermine the value of elite surveys; the data can still answer questions "about trends, the relationship of beliefs to each other, and of beliefs to respondent attributes" (Holsti 1990a, 4). "As a consequence," Holsti writes,

> the issues of whether media leaders should represent X percent or Y percent of the entire sample or whether it should include more business leaders than military officers—or vice versa—are not especially urgent. It is more important that the sample include representatives of many, if not all, major components of the nation's leadership structure and that there be enough respondents in occupational and other sub-categories to permit reliable comparisons among them. The sampling procedures were intended to satisfy these requirements. (Holsti 1990a, 4–5)

A second assumption is also inherent in Holsti and Rosenau's sampling procedures. As Holsti writes,

> Having eschewed the task of constructing a precise replica of America's leadership structure does not, however, imply that the sample is free of premises about American society. For example, the procedures used here clearly incorporate the pluralistic assumption that the foreign policy process in the United States is sensitive to a multiplicity of influences rather than merely to those of a narrow class or sector of society (e.g., business interests). (1990a, 5)

Not surprisingly, then, Holsti and Rosenau sampled a broad spectrum of opinion leaders—ranging from business people and clergy to State Department officials and military officers. And their sample incorporates, but is not limited to, the foreign policy establishment (i.e., people with an expertise and/or influence in foreign policy).

More specifically, the FPLP sample is a composite of nine subsamples: one large sample—approximately 1,800 leaders randomly selected from *Who's Who in America*[5]—and eight smaller samples of approximately 250 leaders each drawn from a variety of more specialized sampling frames. These smaller samples are groups that Holsti and Rosenau felt were underrepresented in *Who's Who in America,* which has a high concentration of business executives and academics; they targeted women, politicians, clergy, State Department officials, labor officials, foreign policy experts outside government, military officers, and media leaders.[6]

In March 1988, Holsti and Rosenau mailed a questionnaire with more than two hundred closed-ended questions to their sample. They followed up two months later with a second mailing to those individuals who had not yet responded.[7] Their response rate was approximately 57 percent (Holsti 1990a, 7).

Adding a Second Wave in 1992

The task of adding a second wave to a preexisting cross-sectional survey is simple if, first, the respondents from the original survey were guaranteed confidentiality but not anonymity, and if, second, the researcher knew and kept records about whether a particular questionnaire came from a particular person.[8] Neither of these conditions obtained for the 1988 FPLP survey. Hence, I was forced to overcome two obstacles: (1) the procedural issue of how to identify individuals in order to link their responses at time 1 with their responses at time 2; (2) the ethical concern of how to protect the respondents' anonymity in the process (Murray 1992).

The Identification Procedure

Two conditions made it possible for me to identify a substantial portion of the respondents from the 1988 FPLP sample.[9] First, Holsti and Rosenau provided me with their mailing list: it included the names of everyone who had been contacted in 1988. (It is important to underscore that the mailing list, alone, provides no clue about whether a particular person filled out a particular questionnaire, or even if he or she returned a questionnaire at all.) Second, I was able to collect demographic information for most of these individuals from published directories.

A large portion of the composite 1988 FPLP sample was drawn

from directories that included biographical information about the individuals (e.g., *Who's Who in America*) and/or was drawn from populations of leaders who were likely to have their biographical descriptions published somewhere. Once I had gathered the demographic characteristics of all the individuals on the mailing list for a particular sample (remember that the 1988 FPLP mailing list consists of nine subsamples), I could then pinpoint which respondents had unique demographic profiles. The identifiable respondents were not unusual by any objective standards: they only had to be unique within that particular sample. If any two people within a given sample had exactly the same demographic profile, I could not discern whether one or the other filled out a particular questionnaire.

For two of the smaller samples—the military officers and labor officials—it was impossible to locate sufficient biographical information. But the FPLP data collection and coding procedures enabled me to know the sampling frame from which a particular respondent was drawn, so these two small samples could be excised from the 1988 data and from the second wave without affecting the other seven samples. By necessity, then, I excluded those military officers and labor officials who were drawn from sampling frames other than *Who's Who in America*.

Protecting the Respondents' Anonymity

This identification procedure, of course, makes it possible to violate the respondents' anonymity if adequate safeguards are not taken. My goal was to create a data set that linked individuals' responses at time 1 with their responses at time 2. A person's name per se is not needed to do this; a subject code will suffice. A simple division of labor was used to preserve the anonymity of the respondents. I identified the respondents within the original sample and joined the first-wave data with the second-wave data, using subject codes assigned by another party. This person never had access to the survey data. I, by contrast, had access to survey responses but not to names.[10]

Let me be more specific about how this task was accomplished. To begin with, I gathered the demographic data for everyone on the original mailing list (where possible), using biographical directories. I then coded this information onto a computer disk. It is important to emphasize that this computer disk contained only the names and addresses from the mailing list and demographic information as derived from published sources; all this information was collected without any reference to the 1988 FPLP survey responses.

The only copy of this disk was given to my colleague, who assigned a random number for each person on the mailing list. He then gave me another disk that contained only the assigned codes and the corresponding demographic characteristics—*but no names*. In short, I now possessed a computer disk that contained only demographic information and subject codes for the leaders originally contacted in 1988.

With this disk, I could now identify leaders who had completed their questionnaires in 1988, and I could do so without knowledge of their names. Using the demographic information gathered from published directories, I pinpointed that subset of individuals from the original mailing list who possessed unique background characteristics.[11] I then matched these individuals against the demographic characteristics as reported by 1988 FPLP respondents on their questionnaires.

After pinpointing the identifiable respondents, I made a note of the corresponding subject codes, and then gave a list of these codes back to my collaborator. He in turn gave me a list of the names and addresses—without codes or demographic characteristics—to include on the mailing list for the 1992 wave. I mailed a lengthy questionnaire to the identifiable respondents in February 1992 and followed up with a second mailing two months later to those who had not responded.[12] The questionnaire itself included sixty-three questions repeated from the earlier FPLP questionnaire and others that were similarly worded; it also included some questions from the 1990 Chicago Council on Foreign Relations (CCFR) questionnaire. The response rate was quite high, at 84 percent.

Once the data from the 1988 wave were attached to those from the 1992 wave, my colleague's disk—the only one that linked names, addresses, codes, and demographic characteristics—was erased. I want to emphasize again that Holsti and Rosenau's original guarantee of anonymity to the FPLP respondents was honored throughout this procedure. No one ever knew how particular leaders answered questions on the FPLP questionnaire or on the LOP questionnaire. This unusual procedure was quite burdensome. But it permitted the construction of a unique panel data set, and, most important, absolutely no harm was done to the participants in the process.

The Introduction of Bias?

Some may suspect that my identification procedure may have skewed the resulting LOP panel data. After all, the process of pinpointing respondents who were unique within the original FPLP samples cannot be viewed as random; in effect, the procedure involved eliminating any FPLP respondents with duplicate demographic profiles from the second wave.[13]

But a comparison of the panel members with the rest of the original

FPLP respondents demonstrates that such concerns are misplaced. Two different types of information are available: first, we know the *demographic characteristics* of all the original respondents and of the portion included in the panel; second, we can compare the panel members' *responses* in the first wave to the responses of the other respondents in the original cross-sectional survey.

Table A.1 allows a comparison of the panel members' demographic characteristics. The first column (labeled *A*) presents demographic data for all of the 1988 FPLP respondents ($N = 1969$).[14] The second column (labeled *B*) and third column (labeled *C*) split the respondents into two subgroups: the panel members ($N = 660$) and the nonpanel respondents ($N = 1309$). We can see from the table that the proportion of men and women, and Republicans and Democrats, remains almost constant between groups. For most occupational categories, the differences are also small, although a somewhat lower percentage of State Department officials and media leaders and a slightly higher percentage of leaders employed in health care are represented within the panel. A higher percentage of the panel members has graduate degrees and has served in the armed forces, but again these differences are not large. Overall, the demographics of the panel members appear remarkably similar to those of the original FPLP sample and its nonpanel members.

Figures A.1 through A.3 present a final piece of demographic data: namely, the comparative distribution of the year of birth for all the

TABLE A.1.   A Comparison of the Demographic Characteristics of All FPLP Respondents, Nonpanel Respondents, and Panel Members (in percentages)

	Group			Differences	
Demographic Characteristics	FPLP (A)	Nonpanel (B)	Panel (C)	A − C	B − C
Occupation:					
Business executives	18.2	17.4	19.8	−1.6	−2.4
Labor officials	0.5	0.8	0.0	0.5	0.8
Educators	30.9	30.4	31.8	−0.9	−1.4
Clergy	5.3	5.0	5.8	−0.5	−0.7
Military officers	1.1	1.0	1.2	−0.1	−0.2
Public officials	5.4	5.1	6.1	−0.6	−0.9
State Department officials	5.5	7.1	2.4	3.1	4.7
Communications	10.2	11.5	7.4	2.7	4.1
Lawyers	6.7	6.1	7.9	−1.2	−1.8
Health care	5.3	4.2	7.4	−2.1	−3.2
Other	8.7	8.7	8.8	−0.1	−0.1
More than one/no answer	2.2	2.6	1.4	0.8	1.2

(Continued)

TABLE A.1. *Continued*

Demographic Characteristics	Group FPLP (A)	Group Nonpanel (B)	Group Panel (C)	Differences A − C	Differences B − C
Sex:					
Men	85.2	84.9	85.8	−0.6	−0.9
Women	13.6	13.4	13.9	−0.4	−0.6
No answer	1.3	1.8	0.3	1.0	1.5
Political Party Preference:					
Republican	29.5	28.6	31.2	−1.7	−2.6
Democrat	39.4	38.8	40.6	−1.2	−1.8
Independent	27.2	28.0	25.8	1.5	2.2
Other	0.7	0.8	0.5	0.3	0.4
No preference	1.9	2.0	1.7	0.2	0.3
No answer	1.3	1.8	0.3	1.0	1.5
Military Service:					
Veteran of military service	48.7	45.8	54.5	−5.8	−8.8
No military service	49.2	51.4	44.7	4.5	6.7
No answer	2.1	2.8	0.8	1.4	2.1
Ideology:					
Far left	0.7	0.6	0.8	−0.1	−0.1
Very liberal	7.7	7.6	8.0	−0.3	−0.5
Somewhat liberal	27.6	27.5	27.9	−0.3	−0.4
Moderate	26.7	27.3	25.6	1.1	1.7
Somewhat conservative	27.0	26.4	28.0	−1.1	−1.6
Very conservative	7.4	7.3	7.6	−0.2	−0.2
Far right	0.2	0.1	0.3	−0.2	−0.2
Other	0.9	0.9	0.8	0.1	0.2
Not sure, no answer	1.9	2.3	1.1	0.8	1.2
Highest Level of Education:					
Some high school	0.3	0.4	0.0	0.3	0.4
High school graduate	0.6	0.3	1.1	−0.5	−0.8
Some college	4.0	4.7	2.6	1.4	2.1
College graduate	10.3	11.3	8.3	2.0	3.0
Some graduate work	10.7	11.8	8.3	2.3	3.5
Graduate degree	73.1	69.9	79.4	−6.3	−9.5
No answer	1.2	1.6	0.3	0.9	1.3
Graduate Degrees:					
MA or MS	16.0	16.7	14.5	1.5	2.2
Ph.D.	32.6	31.9	34.1	−1.5	−2.2
MD or DDS	4.4	3.3	6.5	−2.1	−3.2
LLB or JD	10.2	8.8	13.0	−2.8	−4.2
MBA	3.5	2.8	4.8	−1.3	−2.0
Advanced religious degrees	3.1	3.0	3.5	−0.3	−0.5
Other	0.9	1.1	0.5	0.4	0.6
More than one degree	2.1	2.1	2.3	−0.1	−0.2
No answer	27.2	30.4	20.8	6.4	9.6

Sources: The 1988 FPLP data and the LOP panel data.
Note: The percentages in different demographic categories may not total one hundred due to rounding.

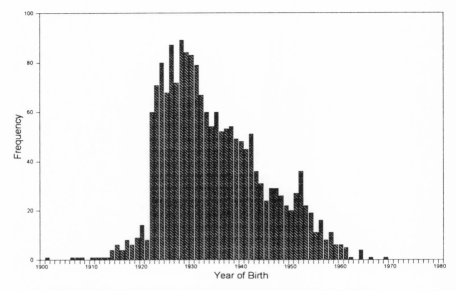

Fig. A.1. Age distribution, all FPLP respondents. (Data from FPLP.)

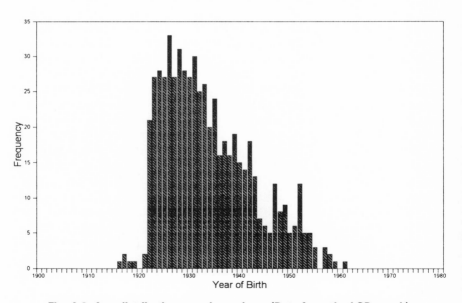

Fig. A.2. Age distribution, panel members. (Data from the LOP panel.)

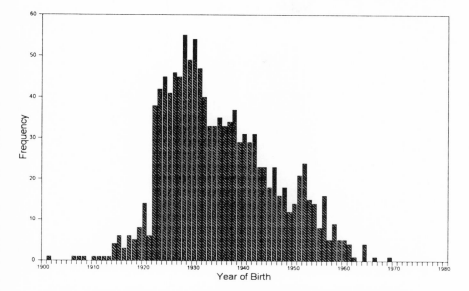

Fig. A.3. Age distribution, nonpanel respondents. (Data from FPLP and the LOP panel.)

FPLP respondents, for the panel members, and for the nonpanel respondents. We can see that the shapes of the histograms are almost identical. The only obvious difference is the few individuals who were born before 1915, apparent in figures A.1 and A.3, are missing from figure A.2.

Now let us compare the three groups using the FPLP 1988 response data. There are approximately two hundred closed-ended questions on the 1988 FPLP questionnaire, each of which has between two and six possible response options: altogether, there are 848 items, not including questions about background characteristics, from which to obtain response frequencies. Once these frequencies were represented as percentages, I subtracted the percentages derived for one group from the percentages derived for another group.

The distribution of the differences in the percentages between the panel members and all the FPLP respondents is shown in figure A.4. On 662 items (78 percent) the difference was one percentage point or less, and on 831 items (98 percent) the difference was three percentage points or less. Only seventeen items (2 percent) fell outside that range, with the greatest difference at six percentage points.

When the panel members were compared to the nonpanel portion, as shown in figure A.5, the distribution was only slightly more dispersed: on 773 items (91 percent) the difference was three percentage points or

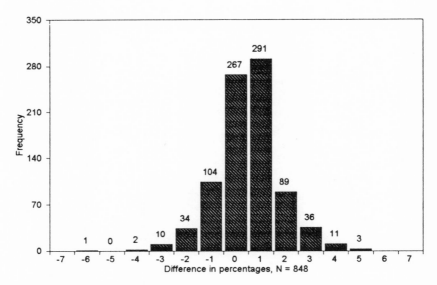

Fig. A.4. Responses of panel members compared to those of all FPLP respondents. (Data from FPLP and the LOP panel.)

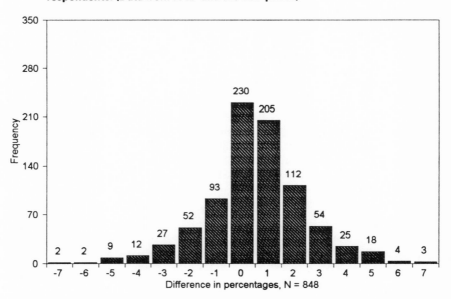

Fig. A.5. Responses of panel members compared to those of nonpanel portion. (Data from FPLP and the LOP panel.)

less; on 810 items (96 percent) it was four percentage points or less; only thirty-eight items (5 percent) fall outside this range, with the greatest difference at seven percentage points. Overall, the panel members' responses in the 1988 wave appear remarkably similar to those from the entire sample and to those from the nonpanel respondents.

As a final check, I compared the responses of panel members with those of the nonpanel portion using a difference of means test. Only 5 percent of the questions revealed a statistically significant difference between the two groups at the .05 level.[15] And, even on these few questions, the difference in the means between the two groups was quite small: the average difference in means was .11 for the four-point questions (that is, the questions in which the scores ranged from 1 to 4) and .09 for the three-point questions.

Fortunately, then, the identification procedure used to add a second wave does not appear to have skewed the results. It is true that some demographic characteristics, such as military service and graduate degrees, aided in the identification process and that such people have a somewhat higher representation in the panel. But, again, the differences are small. And the distribution of responses given by the panel members on the 1988 questionnaire is quite close to those given by all FPLP respondents and by the nonpanel members.

APPENDIX B

The Value of Panel Data

The two major sources of trend survey data on foreign policy—the Chicago Council on Foreign Relations (CCFR) and the Foreign Policy Leadership Project (FPLP)—have surveyed American opinion leaders every four years since the mid-1970s.[1] Both studies provide longitudinal data that spans the period before and after the end of the Cold War. With this wealth of survey research, what additional insights can the Leadership Opinion Project (LOP) panel data offer?

Sequential cross-sectional studies suffer some limitations for assessing the dynamics of opinion change; they can only measure net change in opinion, not the number, direction, and character of individual shifts in opinion that, when aggregated, make up the net changes.[2] Trend studies draw different samples from the same (or comparable) population at regular time intervals. In contrast, panel studies observe the same individuals more than once. Both research methods permit the measurement of changes in a particular variable between time periods but at different levels of analysis. With cross-sectional data, the researcher observes changes within a particular population or subgroup; with panel data, the researcher also tracks changes at the individual level (Baltes and Nesselroade 1979; Babbie 1990; Menard 1991).

The investigative power of the panel research design can be illustrated by referring to the composition of a turnover table. A turnover table is a means for showing how panel participants respond to the same question at two points in time; table B.1 provides a guide for reading these tables. With trend data, *researchers possess the equivalent of the column and row marginals on the outside of the table:* that is, they know what percentage of the total sample agreed and disagreed with proposition x at time 1 and at time 2. (Of course, with actual trend data these group percentages would be derived from two or more samples, whereas the marginals in a turnover table are derived from one sample over time.) *But what is remarkable about panel data is that we can see inside the table as well; we can actually observe whether individuals gave the same or different responses when asked a particular question over time.*

Consequently, the LOP panel data can provide a much fuller account

TABLE B.1. Illustration of How to Read a Turnover Table

Same Individuals' Opinions at Time 2 (Rows)	Individuals' Opinions at Time 1 (Columns)		
	Agree	Disagree	
Agree	(A) Individuals whose opinions stay stable: they agree both at T1 and T2	(B) Individuals whose opinions change: they disagree at T1 but agree at T2	(A+B) Percentage of total sample who agree at T2
Disagree	(C) Individuals whose opinions change: they agree at T1 but disagree at T2	(D) Individuals whose opinions stay stable: they disagree both at T1 and T2	(C+D) Percentage of total sample who disagree at T2
	(A+C) Percentage of total sample who agree at T1	(B+D) Percentage of total sample who disagree at T1	(A+B+C+D) Total

of the stability or instability of leaders' attitudes following the end of the Cold War. An additional illustration will make this point clear. Table B.2 presents a hypothetical example which illustrates that substantial change among individuals can be disguised within aggregated data found in trend studies. Notice first that the net percentage of the sample who agreed and disagreed with proposition *x* remained constant: as seen in the marginals, 60 percent agreed and 40 percent disagreed at both time points. But the cell frequencies inside the table tell a very different story: here we can see that 30 percent of the respondents had shifted from agreement to disagreement with proposition *x* between time 1 and time 2 (quadrant *C*), and another 30 percent had shifted in the opposite direction (quadrant *B*). In other words, this example shows that if individuals shift their opinions in opposing directions, they can cancel each other out, and their movement can be concealed within aggregated data.

Another important advantage of using panel data rather than trend data is that we possess information about respondents' prior beliefs. Returning to our hypothetical example, panel data allow us to easily observe the relationship between respondents' answers at time 1 and their answers at time 2 using column percentages (see table B.3): 50 percent of those respondents who had agreed with proposition *x* at time 1 shifted to disagreement by time 2 (quadrant *C*); 75 percent of those respondents who had disagreed with proposition *x* at time 1 shifted to agreement by time 2 (quadrant *B*). Because trend studies are a compilation of different cross-sectional samples, direct information about respondents' past views is unavailable: researchers can ask respondents to recall what they believed in the past, but self-reported recollections are not as reliable.

Finally, panel data permit us to investigate whether dynamic

TABLE B.2.   Hypothetical Example of Individual-Level Change and Aggregate-Level Stability in Attitudes, Turnover Table

		Time 1 (Columns) Agree	Disagree	
Time 2 (Rows)	Agree	(A) 30%	(B) 30%	(A+B) 60%
	Disagree	(C) 30%	(D) 10%	(C+D) 40%
		60% (A+C)	40% (B+D)	100% (A+B+C+D)

TABLE B.3. Hypothetical Example of Individual-Level Change in Attitudes Using Column Percentages, Turnover Table

| | | Time 1 (Columns) | |
		Agree	Disagree
Time 2 (Rows)	Agree	(A) 50%	(B) 75%
	Disagree	(C) 50%	(D) 25%
		100% (A+C)	100% (B+D)

constraint exists between different attitudinal variables. More specifically, the panel research design allows us to test whether a change in attitude x within individuals' belief systems is accompanied by a change in attitude y. Those rare panel studies that bracket key historical events (such as the LOP study) are especially valuable in this regard: if outside stimuli (such as the end of the Cold War) provoke respondents to reevaluate their beliefs, then researchers can untangle the interconnections between the attitudes that exhibit change (e.g., views about the threat posed by Russia) and other attitudes (e.g., stances toward the use of force).

To sum up, only panel data allow us to observe whether stability in group percentages reflects actual stability among individuals, to compare individuals' past beliefs with their more current views, and to observe the dynamic interrelationships between attitudes within individuals' belief systems.

APPENDIX C

Measures and Reliability

The Construction of Indexes

To reduce the effects of random measurement error, I used summated rating scales (Spector 1992). I rescaled individual question items to range from zero to one, reversing the polarity of some questions as necessary, and then calculated the respondents' average score. Whenever possible, I used repeated question items and constructed the indexes in pairs—one for 1988 and one for 1992—so that they can be compared over time.

There are at least three alternative methods for treating missing data. First, one can use list-wise deletion, that is, drop all the cases with any missing data from the analyses. Second, one can calculate the respondents' average score for a particular belief using those responses that are available. Let us say, for instance, that a particular index is constructed out of four questions: in most cases, the respondents' average scores would be calculated using those four questions; in some cases, however, the average score would be calculated from only three or two of the questions. Third, one can replace the missing data with the sample mean for that question item.

I chose the latter approach. It is important to note, however, that the substantive results are not affected by this choice. I ran the various analyses using the other techniques for dealing with missing data, and the results did not change; indeed, they were often slightly improved.

Finally, I used the Cronbach alpha as a test of the internal consistency of the indexes: in almost every instance, the coefficient was well above the standard cutoff point of .70 (Spector 1992; Nunnally 1978).

Militant Internationalism (MI88, MI92): This pair of scales, constructed from four repeated question items (see table C.1), taps respondents' general beliefs about the use of military instruments of power.[1]

The indexes are anchored at one end by respondents who advocated the assertive use of U.S. military force abroad—they could score as low as zero—and at the other end by people who contested the use of force—they could score as high as one.

The Cronbach alpha scores for these scales were high by the standards of survey data: .78 for MI88 and .71 for MI92.

Cooperative Internationalism (CI88, CI92):   This pair of scales, constructed from seven repeated questions (see table C.1), measure respondents' attitudes about U.S. involvement in cooperative ventures abroad.

A person who strongly advocated U.S. activism in cooperative ventures with other countries would score at or near one; a person who strongly disagreed with such involvement would score at or near zero.

The internal consistency of these scales was high. The Cronbach alpha was .80 for both CI88 and CI92.

Containment (COMM88, COMM92):   This pair of scales, created from four repeated questions (see table C.1), taps respondents' beliefs about the containment of communism.

The polarity of the scales is as follows: those respondents highly concerned about the threat of communism would score at or near zero; those not at all concerned would score at or near one.

The Cronbach alpha for COMM88 was .86; for COMM92 it was .75.

Images of Russia (SU88, RUS92):   Because the Soviet Union collapsed, it was impossible to use repeated questions to measure leaders' perceptions of that country over time. Instead, I created one index (SU88) to measure respondents' beliefs about whether the Soviet Union was an expansionist power using three questions from the 1988 questionnaire; then I created a separate index (RUS92) using two similar questions asked about Russia in 1992 (see table C.1).

The polarity in these scales is as follows: respondents who perceived the Soviet Union or Russia as highly aggressive would score at or near zero; those who considered the Soviet Union or Russia to be a nonexpansionist, status quo power would reside at or near one.

The Cronbach alpha was high at .80 for SU88. However, the correlation between the two questions used to construct the RUS92 scale was .40, suggesting that respondents were no longer as sure about their views toward Russia.

Attitudes about Domestic Policy (DOM88, DOM92):   The last pair of scales, created from five repeated questions, measures respondents' attitudes toward domestic policy (see table C.1).

TABLE C.1. Question Items and Reliability of Scales

Index Name	Wave	Cronbach Alpha	Questions	Type
MI88 MI92	1988 1992	0.78 0.71	There is nothing wrong with using the CIA to try to undermine hostile governments [reversed]	A
			The conduct of American foreign affairs relies excessively on military advice	A
			Military aid programs will eventually draw the United States into unnecessary wars	A
			Military superiority of the United States (as an approach to world peace) [reversed]	C
CI88 CI92	1988 1992	0.80 0.80	Fostering international cooperation to solve common problems, such as food, inflation and energy (as a U.S. foreign policy goal)	B
			Combating world hunger (as a U.S. foreign policy goal)	B
			Helping to improve the standard of living in less-developed countries (as a U.S. foreign policy goal)	B
			Protecting the global environment (as a U.S. foreign policy goal)	B
			Worldwide arms control (as a U.S. foreign policy goal)	B
			The United States should give economic aid to poorer countries even if it means higher prices at home	A
			Strengthening the UN and other international organizations (as an approach to world peace)	C
COMM88 COMM92	1988 1992	0.86 0.75	There is considerable validity in the domino theory that when one nation falls to communism, others nearby will soon follow a similar path [reversed]	A
			Any communist victory is a defeat for America's national interest [reversed]	A
			The United States should take all steps including the use of force to prevent the spread of communism [reversed]	A
			Containing communism (as a U.S. foreign policy goal) [reversed]	
SU88	1988	0.80	Soviet foreign policy goals are inherently expansionist and will not change until there is a fundamental transformation of the Soviet system [reversed]	A

(Continued)

TABLE C.1. *Continued*

Index Name	Wave	Cronbach Alpha	Questions	Type
			The Soviet Union is generally expansionist rather than defensive in its foreign policy goals [reversed]	A
			The Soviet invasion of Afghanistan was one step in a larger plan to control the Persian Gulf area [reversed]	A
RUS92	1992	0.40 [Pearson *r*]	Once their economy stabilizes, Russia will become an expansionist military power [reversed]	A
			Russia poses no threat to Western Europe or the United States	A
DOM88	1988	0.75	Permitting prayer in schools	A
DOM92	1992	0.76	[reversed]	
			Relaxing environmental regulation to stimulate economic growth [reversed]	A
			Barring homosexuals from teaching in public schools [reversed]	A
			Redistributing income from the wealthy to the poor through taxation and subsidies	A
			Banning the death penalty	A

Note: A = Four-point scale ranging from "agree strongly" to "disagree strongly."
B = Three-point scale using "very important," "important," and "not important."
C = Four-point scale ranging from "very effective" to "not at all effective."

Respondents with a conservative orientation toward domestic policy would reside at the low end of the scale and those with a liberal orientation at the high end.

The Cronbach alpha for these scales was again high at .75 for DOM88 and .76 for DOM92.

Additional Variables Used

Ideology: Respondents were asked, "How would you describe your views on political matters?" They could answer in nine possible ways: "far left," "very liberal," "somewhat liberal," "moderate," "somewhat conservative," "very conservative," "far right," "other," and "not sure." I treated those who answered "other" or "not sure" as missing data and replaced these data points with the sample mean. The other responses were scaled such that "far right" equaled zero and "far left" equaled one.

Generation: Although generational experiences cannot be measured directly with the LOP data, we can use respondents' years of birth as a proxy for generational experiences (Holsti and Rosenau 1980). Three dummy variables were used: respondents born before 1924 were included in the "WWII" generation; respondents born between 1924 and 1932 were included in the "Korea" generation; respondents born since 1940 were included in the "Vietnam" generation. In each case, if a respondent was a member of the generation in question, he or she would receive a score of one; all others would receive a score of zero.

Gender: Males are given a score of zero, females a score of one. In this instance, cases with missing data were eliminated from the analyses.

Military service: Those who served in the military are given a score of zero, and those who did not are given a score of one. Cases with missing data were eliminated from the analyses.

APPENDIX D

American Opinion Leaders and U.S. Foreign Policy

Do you think the United States plays a more important and powerful role as a world leader today compared to ten years ago, about as important a role, or a less important role as a world leader than it did ten years ago? Please check **only one** box.

☐ More important

☐ As important

☐ Less important

Some people say that America has been unable to solve its economic problems and that this has caused the country to decline as a world power. Do you agree or disagree with this view?

☐ Agree

☐ Disagree

Here is a list of possible threats to the vital interests of the United States in the next ten years. For each item, please indicate whether you see this as a critical threat, an important but not critical threat, or not an important threat at all. Please check **only one** box in each row.

	Critical	Important	Not Important
The economic power of Japan	☐	☐	☐
Economic competition from Europe	☐	☐	☐
The development of China as a world power	☐	☐	☐
The military power of Russia	☐	☐	☐
Instability in the former Soviet Union	☐	☐	☐
Economic problems in the United States (unemployment, inflation, etc.)	☐	☐	☐
Social order problems in the United States (crime, drugs, etc.)	☐	☐	☐
Proliferation of nuclear weapons	☐	☐	☐
Environmental problems	☐	☐	☐
Regional conflicts in the Third World	☐	☐	☐
Other (please specify) _____	☐	☐	☐

This question asks you to indicate your position on certain government programs. Please indicate whether you believe the amount spent on each program should be increased, kept about the same, or decreased by checking **only one** box in each row.

	Increase Substantially	*Increase Slightly*	*Keep the Same*	*Decrease Slightly*	*Decrease Substantially*
Aid to education	☐	☐	☐	☐	☐
Defense spending	☐	☐	☐	☐	☐
Social security	☐	☐	☐	☐	☐
Military aid to other nations	☐	☐	☐	☐	☐
Economic aid to other nations	☐	☐	☐	☐	☐
Welfare and relief programs at home	☐	☐	☐	☐	☐
The C.I.A.'s budget	☐	☐	☐	☐	☐

Here are a few statements about the extent of changes in Russia. Please indicate how strongly you agree or disagree with each statement by checking **only one** box in each row.

	Agree Strongly	*Agree Somewhat*	*Disagree Somewhat*	*Disagree Strongly*	*No Opinion*
There has been a fundamental transformation in Russia from an authoritarian and communist society to a democratic and liberal society	☐	☐	☐	☐	☐
Recent changes notwithstanding, Russian foreign and domestic policy is essentially guided by Marxist-Leninist ideology	☐	☐	☐	☐	☐
Communist leaders still retain enormous influence in the formulation of foreign and domestic policy in Russia	☐	☐	☐	☐	☐
The failure of the August coup demonstrates the strength of democratic leaders in Russia	☐	☐	☐	☐	☐
Although Russia has become much more democratic, it is quite likely that conservatives will one day regain power	☐	☐	☐	☐	☐
Authoritarianism is an intrinsic part of the Russian national character	☐	☐	☐	☐	☐

This question asks you to indicate your position on certain propositions that are sometimes described as lessons that the United States should have learned from past experiences abroad. Please indicate how strongly you agree or disagree with each statement by checking only **one box** in each row.

	Agree Strongly	Agree Somewhat	Disagree Somewhat	Disagree Strongly	No Opinion
* America's conception of its leadership in the world must be scaled down	☐	☐	☐	☐	☐
* It is vital to enlist the cooperation of the U.N. in settling international disputes	☐	☐	☐	☐	☐
* There is considerable validity in the "domino theory" that when one nation falls to communism, others nearby will soon follow a similar path	☐	☐	☐	☐	☐
The free-enterprise system is the best model for the world	☐	☐	☐	☐	☐
* Military aid programs will eventually draw the United States into unnecessary wars	☐	☐	☐	☐	☐
It is necessary to use military force to stop aggression; economic sanctions are not enough	☐	☐	☐	☐	☐
Recent events in the Soviet Union and Eastern Europe mean the end of communism as a major force in the world	☐	☐	☐	☐	☐
* The United States is generally expansionist rather than defensive in its foreign policy goals	☐	☐	☐	☐	☐
* Any communist victory is a defeat for America's national interest	☐	☐	☐	☐	☐
* When force is used, military rather than political goals should determine its application	☐	☐	☐	☐	☐

This question asks you to choose between the following two scenarios. Which scenario would you prefer to see happen over the next ten years?

☐ The U.S. economy grows at 2.5% a year while the European Community's economy grows at 6.5% a year

☐ The U.S. economy grows at 1% a year while the European Community's economy grows at 1.1% a year

*   Repeated question

Here are some statements about Soviet foreign policy. Please indicate how strongly you agree or disagree with each statement by checking **only one** box in each row.

	Agree Strongly	Agree Somewhat	Disagree Somewhat	Disagree Strongly	No Opinion
Soviet foreign policy was essentially guided by Marxist-Leninist ideology	☐	☐	☐	☐	☐
Soviet foreign policy goals did not differ significantly from those of all major powers	☐	☐	☐	☐	☐
The Soviets sought to expand only when the risks of doing so were relatively low	☐	☐	☐	☐	☐
Soviet foreign policy actions often stemmed from genuine fears for Russian security	☐	☐	☐	☐	☐
The Soviet Union was generally expansionist rather than defensive in its foreign policy goals	☐	☐	☐	☐	☐
The Gorbachev regime in the USSR sincerely sought to stabilize relations with the United States	☐	☐	☐	☐	☐
* The Soviet invasion of Afghanistan was one step in a larger plan to control the Persian Gulf area	☐	☐	☐	☐	☐

Turning to issues closer to home, if government spending on defense is greatly reduced, do you think this will hurt the economy in your local area, help the economy in your local area, or won't it make any difference to the economy in your local area?

☐ Hurt the local economy   ☐ Make no difference

☐ Help the local economy   ☐ No opinion

If government spending on defense is greatly reduced, do you think this will hurt your household's financial position, help your household's financial position, or won't it make any difference to your household's financial position?

☐ Hurt household   ☐ Make no difference

☐ Help household   ☐ No opinion

Please indicate how strongly you agree or disagree with each of the following statements concerning America's role in the world. Please check **only one** box in each row.

	Agree Strongly	Agree Somewhat	Disagree Somewhat	Disagree Strongly	No Opinion
* The United States has a moral obligation to prevent the destruction of the state of Israel	☐	☐	☐	☐	☐
* There is nothing wrong with using the C.I.A. to try to undermine hostile governments	☐	☐	☐	☐	☐
* We shouldn't think so much in international terms but concentrate more on our own national problems	☐	☐	☐	☐	☐
* The United States should give economic aid to poorer countries even if it means higher prices at home	☐	☐	☐	☐	☐
* The United States should take all steps including the use of force to prevent the spread of communism	☐	☐	☐	☐	☐
There is nothing wrong with the United States unilaterally using military force abroad	☐	☐	☐	☐	☐
* The United States should support creation of a homeland for Palestinians	☐	☐	☐	☐	☐
The United States should take a more active role in supporting democratic principles abroad	☐	☐	☐	☐	☐
The highest priority of American foreign policy should be the enhancement of our national power	☐	☐	☐	☐	☐
The United States should not meddle in other countries' domestic affairs	☐	☐	☐	☐	☐
The United States may have to support some dictators because they are friendly toward us	☐	☐	☐	☐	☐

Do you think we should expand our spending on national defense over the next five years, keep it about the same, or cut back?

☐ Expand   ☐ Cut back moderately (15% - 30%)

☐ Keep it about the same   ☐ Cut back substantially (30% - 45%)

☐ Cut back slightly (less than 15%)   ☐ Cut back deeply (45% or more)

How much importance do you attach to each of the following as a cause of war. Please indicate your assessment by checking **only one** box in each row.

	Very Important	Moderately Important	Slightly Important	Not at All Important	Not Sure
* Human nature (aggressive, irrational, selfish, etc.)	☐	☐	☐	☐	☐
* Aggressive nations that seek to dominate others	☐	☐	☐	☐	☐
* Particular leaders (Napoleon, Hitler, Stalin, etc.)	☐	☐	☐	☐	☐
* Nationalism	☐	☐	☐	☐	☐
* An international system in which there is no central authority to settle disputes	☐	☐	☐	☐	☐
* Ideology	☐	☐	☐	☐	☐
* Ignorance, misunderstanding and inadequate communication among peoples	☐	☐	☐	☐	☐
* Power politics	☐	☐	☐	☐	☐
* Economic rivalries among nations	☐	☐	☐	☐	☐

How effective do you consider each of the following as an approach to world peace. Please indicate your assessment by checking **only one** box in each row.

	Very Effective	Moderately Effective	Slightly Effective	Not at All Effective	Not Sure
* Military superiority of the United States	☐	☐	☐	☐	☐
* Collective security through alliances	☐	☐	☐	☐	☐
* Trade, technical cooperation, and economic interdependence	☐	☐	☐	☐	☐
* Arms control	☐	☐	☐	☐	☐
* Narrowing the gap between rich and poor nations	☐	☐	☐	☐	☐
* Strengthening the U.N. and other international organizations	☐	☐	☐	☐	☐
* Political efforts to achieve a balance of power within regions and between the major powers	☐	☐	☐	☐	☐
* Better communication and understanding among peoples and nations	☐	☐	☐	☐	☐

This question asks you to indicate your position on additional propositions that are sometimes described as lessons that the United States should have learned from past experiences abroad. Please indicate how strongly you agree or disagree with each statement by checking **only one** box in each row.

	Agree Strongly	Agree Somewhat	Disagree Somewhat	Disagree Strongly	No Opinion
* The efficiency of military power in foreign affairs is declining	☐	☐	☐	☐	☐
Detente permitted the USSR to pursue policies that promoted rather than restrained conflict	☐	☐	☐	☐	☐
* The conduct of American foreign affairs relies excessively on military advice	☐	☐	☐	☐	☐
The United States, at great cost to herself, has promoted the cause of democracy abroad	☐	☐	☐	☐	☐
* Revolutionary forces in the Third World are usually nationalist rather than controlled by the USSR or China	☐	☐	☐	☐	☐
* Stationing American troops abroad encourages other countries to let us do their fighting for them	☐	☐	☐	☐	☐
The United States should undertake military intervention in the Middle East in the event of another threat to the oil supply	☐	☐	☐	☐	☐
* The United States should bring home all its troops stationed in Europe	☐	☐	☐	☐	☐
There was no moral difference between the Soviet Union and the United States during the Cold War; all superpowers seek to enhance their direct interests	☐	☐	☐	☐	☐

Here are a list of defense programs. Please indicate whether you believe the amount spent on each program should be increased, kept at current levels, or decreased by checking **only one** box in each row.

	Increase Substantially	Increase Slightly	Keep the Same	Decrease Slightly	Decrease Substantially
The Stealth B-2 bomber	☐	☐	☐	☐	☐
The MX missile	☐	☐	☐	☐	☐
The Midgetman missile	☐	☐	☐	☐	☐
SDI (or Star Wars)	☐	☐	☐	☐	☐

Some people feel that NATO has outlived its usefulness, and that the United States should withdraw militarily from NATO. Others say that NATO still has a function in preserving peace in Europe. Do you feel that we should increase our commitment to NATO, keep our commitment what it is now, decrease our commitment but still remain in NATO, or withdraw from NATO entirely?

☐ Increase commitment   ☐ Decrease commitment

☐ Keep commitment what it is now   ☐ Withdraw commitment

More specifically, there were approximately 300,000 U.S. troops stationed in Western Europe in 1990. How many U.S. troops do you think we should have in Western Europe by 1995? Please check **only one** box.

☐ 350,000 troops   ☐ 150,000 troops

☐ 300,000 troops   ☐ 100,000 troops

☐ 250,000 troops   ☐ 50,000 troops

☐ 200,000 troops   ☐ None

Here is a list of possible reasons for continued U.S. involvement in NATO. Please indicate how strongly you agree or disagree with each reason by checking **only one** box in each row.

	Agree Strongly	Agree Somewhat	Disagree Somewhat	Disagree Strongly	No Opinion
Maintenance of U.S. influence in Europe	☐	☐	☐	☐	☐
Instability in Eastern Europe	☐	☐	☐	☐	☐
Instability in the former Soviet Union	☐	☐	☐	☐	☐
Leaders hostile to the United States and Western Europe might replace Gorbachev and Yeltsin	☐	☐	☐	☐	☐
Distrust of a unified Germany	☐	☐	☐	☐	☐

Other (please specify) _____

Turning to more general considerations, here is a list of possible foreign policy goals that the United States might have. Please indicate how much importance you think should be attached to each goal. Check **only one** box in each row.

	Very Important	Somewhat Important	Not Important at All	Not Sure
Protecting weaker nations against foreign aggression	☐	☐	☐	☐
* Reducing the U.S. trade deficit with foreign countries	☐	☐	☐	☐
* Helping to improve the standard of living in less developed countries	☐	☐	☐	☐
* Worldwide arms control	☐	☐	☐	☐
* Defending our allies' security	☐	☐	☐	☐
* Securing adequate supplies of energy	☐	☐	☐	☐
* Helping to bring a democratic form of government to other nations	☐	☐	☐	☐
* Promoting and defending human rights in other countries	☐	☐	☐	☐
* Combatting world hunger	☐	☐	☐	☐
* Strengthening the United Nations	☐	☐	☐	☐
* Protecting the global environment	☐	☐	☐	☐
* Fostering international cooperation to solve common problems, such as food, inflation, and energy	☐	☐	☐	☐
* Containing communism	☐	☐	☐	☐
* Protecting the jobs of American workers	☐	☐	☐	☐
Protecting the interests of American business abroad	☐	☐	☐	☐

Some people anticipate that the United States and Japan, due to economic tensions, will become adversaries in the next decade. Other people believe that Japan and the United States will continue to be close allies. How friendly do you think our relationship with Japan will be a decade from now?

     ☐ Very friendly   ☐ Not too friendly

     ☐ Somewhat friendly   ☐ Not at all friendly

The following are possible reasons that the Soviet leadership initiated reforms at home and permitted the collapse of the Soviet empire in Eastern Europe. Please rank the following options in order of importance, labelling the most important reason with a number one, the next most important with a two, and so on.

_____   The economic crisis in the Soviet Union

_____   The U.S. military build-up during the Reagan era

_____   A new generation of Soviet leaders with different foreign policy goals

_____   The Western alliance's sustained commitment to contain communism

_____   The failure of communism to provide basic political freedoms

_____   Other (please specify) _____

This question asks you to indicate your position on certain domestic issues. Please indicate how strongly you agree or disagree with each statement by checking **only one** box in each row.

	Agree Strongly	Agree Somewhat	Disagree Somewhat	Disagree Strongly	No Opinion
* Relaxing environmental regulation to stimulate economic growth	☐	☐	☐	☐	☐
Raising income taxes	☐	☐	☐	☐	☐
Establishing national health insurance	☐	☐	☐	☐	☐
* Leaving abortion decisions to women and their doctors	☐	☐	☐	☐	☐
* Permitting prayer in public schools	☐	☐	☐	☐	☐
* Erecting trade barriers against foreign goods to protect American industries and jobs	☐	☐	☐	☐	☐
Reducing the defense budget in order to increase domestic social spending	☐	☐	☐	☐	☐
* Barring homosexuals from teaching in public schools	☐	☐	☐	☐	☐
* Opening up more parks and recreation lands for oil drilling	☐	☐	☐	☐	☐
* Redistributing income from the wealthy to the poor through taxation and subsidies	☐	☐	☐	☐	☐
Reducing the federal budget deficit	☐	☐	☐	☐	☐
* Banning the death penalty	☐	☐	☐	☐	☐

Here is a list of past U.S. foreign and defense policies. Please indicate how strongly you agreed or disagreed with these policies from the 1970s and 1980s by checking **only one** box in each row.

	Agreed Strongly	Agreed Somewhat	Disagreed Somewhat	Disagreed Strongly	No Opinion
* Supporting rebels fighting the Sandinista government in Nicaragua	☐	☐	☐	☐	☐
* Sending military advisors to El Salvador	☐	☐	☐	☐	☐
* Giving high priority to a defense build-up	☐	☐	☐	☐	☐
Sending American troops to Grenada	☐	☐	☐	☐	☐
* Bombing Libya in the spring of 1986	☐	☐	☐	☐	☐
* Preventing American firms from selling non-strategic equipment to the Soviet Union	☐	☐	☐	☐	☐
* Aiding anti-communist rebels in Angola	☐	☐	☐	☐	☐
Mining the Nicaraguan harbors	☐	☐	☐	☐	☐
Placing Pershing missiles in Europe	☐	☐	☐	☐	☐
Pursuing a policy of Detente in the 1970s	☐	☐	☐	☐	☐
Signing the SALT II agreement with the USSR	☐	☐	☐	☐	☐

During the next ten years, which of the following countries do you believe will be the main military adversary of the United States?

☐ China

☐ Germany

☐ Japan

☐ Russia

☐ Iraq

☐ The U.S. will have no main military adversary

☐ Other (please specify) _____

Here is a list of statements about international affairs and U.S. foreign policy for a post-Cold War era. For each, please indicate how strongly you agree or disagree by checking **only one** box in each row.

	Agree Strongly	Agree Somewhat	Disagree Somewhat	Disagree Strongly	No Opinion
Russia poses no threat to Western Europe or the United States	☐	☐	☐	☐	☐
Because the future is uncertain, the United States needs to maintain high levels of defense spending	☐	☐	☐	☐	☐
The CIA's activities should be limited to intelligence gathering	☐	☐	☐	☐	☐
The United States needs to keep ahead of Russia in strategic nuclear weapons	☐	☐	☐	☐	☐
The United States should close most of its foreign military bases	☐	☐	☐	☐	☐
The collapse of the Soviet Union does not mean that the United States can let down its guard; there will always be powerful, aggressive nations in the world	☐	☐	☐	☐	☐
The United States needs to develop SDI to protect against accidental and limited nuclear attacks	☐	☐	☐	☐	☐
Russia and the United States share a number of foreign policy interests such as prevention of war, arms control, and stabilizing relations between them	☐	☐	☐	☐	☐
The collapse of communism means that there will be many more democracies in the world	☐	☐	☐	☐	☐
As the number of democracies in the world increases, international relations will become much more peaceful and harmonious	☐	☐	☐	☐	☐
Once their economic crisis stabilizes, Russia will become an expansionist military power	☐	☐	☐	☐	☐
The United States overextended itself in the fight against communism	☐	☐	☐	☐	☐
The United States should urge Japan and Europe to play a greater leadership role in the world	☐	☐	☐	☐	☐
The economic demise of the United States is greatly exaggerated	☐	☐	☐	☐	☐
The United States can now dismantle most of its strategic nuclear weapons	☐	☐	☐	☐	☐

Here is a list of recent U.S. foreign and defense policies. Please indicate whether you agree or disagree with these policies by checking **only one** box in each row.

	Agree Strongly	Agree Somewhat	Disagree Somewhat	Disagree Strongly	No Opinion
The U.S. military response to the Iraqi invasion of Kuwait	☐	☐	☐	☐	☐
The agreement with the USSR to limit conventional weapons in Europe (CFE Treaty)	☐	☐	☐	☐	☐
The agreement with the USSR to reduce both American and Soviet strategic nuclear weapons (The START Treaty)	☐	☐	☐	☐	☐
The U.S. provision of economic aid and loans to help ease the food crisis in the former Soviet Union this winter	☐	☐	☐	☐	☐
The U.S. intervention in Panama	☐	☐	☐	☐	☐
The U.S. mild response to the Chinese government crackdown on pro-democracy demonstrators	☐	☐	☐	☐	☐

Please indicate if you would favor or oppose the following types of relationships with Russia.

	Favor Strongly	Favor Somewhat	Oppose Somewhat	Oppose Strongly
Sharing technical information about defending against missile attacks	☐	☐	☐	☐
Limiting the sales of advanced U.S. computers	☐	☐	☐	☐
Negotiating arms control agreements	☐	☐	☐	☐
Donating American grain and other farm products	☐	☐	☐	☐
Providing financial loans	☐	☐	☐	☐
Providing cash that would not have to be paid back	☐	☐	☐	☐
Extending NATO membership to Russia	☐	☐	☐	☐

This question asks you to choose again between two scenarios. Which scenario would you prefer to see happen in the next ten years?

☐ The U.S. economy grows at 2.5% a year while Japan's economy grows at 6.5% a year

☐ The U.S. economy grows at 1% a year while Japan's economy grows at 1.1% a year

Here are a few questions for background information.

☐ Male   ☐ Female   Year of Birth: _____

What is the highest level of education that you have completed?

Some High School	High School Graduate	Some College	College Graduate	Some Graduate Work	Graduate Degree	Type of Graduate Degree
☐	☐	☐	☐	☐	☐	_____

Have you earned any type of degree within the last five years? Yes ☐   No ☐
What type of degree?   _____

What is your primary occupation?

☐ Business executive   ☐ Educator   ☐ Military officer

☐ Labor official   ☐ Journalist   ☐ State Department official

☐ Health care   ☐ Communications   ☐ Federal official
                                          (other than State Dept.)
☐ Clergy   ☐ Lawyer   ☐ Local public official

☐ Defense industry   ☐ Scholar at a   ☐ Other
                          research institute

If you answered "business executive" or "labor official," please identify with which industry you are associated: _____

If you answered "business executive," does your firm have business transactions with Russia?

☐ Yes   ☐ No

Do you anticipate that your firm will increase business transactions with Russia in the next decade?

☐ Yes   ☐ No

If you answered "educator," please identify the general area you teach:

☐ Humanities   ☐ Sciences

☐ Social sciences   ☐ Other (please specify) _____

Have you changed occupations in the last five years?   ☐ Yes   ☐ No

If "yes," what was your previous occupation? _____

Have you ever served in the armed forces?   ☐ Yes   ☐ No

Branch of service: _____

How would you describe your views on political matters?

☐ Far left   ☐ Moderate   ☐ Far right
☐ Very liberal   ☐ Somewhat conservative   ☐ Other
☐ Somewhat liberal   ☐ Very conservative   ☐ Not sure

Generally speaking, do you regard yourself as a Republican, a Democrat, an Independent, or what?

☐ Strong Republican   ☐ Weak Democrat   ☐ Other
☐ Weak Republican   ☐ Strong Democrat
☐ Independent   ☐ No preference

Notes

Chapter 1

1. See also May (1973) and Jervis (1976). They both caution decision makers against a common pattern of faulty reasoning: lessons derived from particularly salient international events (such as wars) are often applied to other—and often dissimilar—circumstances.

2. Kritzer (1978, 491), using a 1972 sample of national convention delegates, also reported substantial correlations between scales designed to measure attitudes about foreign affairs and those used to measure domestic issues and ideology. However, Kritzer does not explicitly make this point in his analysis.

3. The idea appears elsewhere as well. For example, Campbell, Converse, Miller, and Stokes ([1960] 1980, 189) argued in *The American Voter* that an "attitude structure" may be said to exist "when two or more beliefs or opinions held by an individual are in some way or another functionally related."

4. See Fiske and Taylor (1984) for a detailed explanation of this concept. Also see the symposium in the December 1991 issue of the *American Political Science Review* for a debate on the usefulness of the term *schema*.

5. Indeed, the same variables that predispose certain individuals to embrace a particular posture may also predispose them to become attached to a particular image of the Soviet Union. Etheredge (1978) found that certain personality traits (e.g., ambition, competitiveness) in policymakers were associated with hard-line attitudes about the use of force and perceptions of the Soviet Union.

6. It is possible, for instance, that the process of belief change involves more social interaction than discussed here. Perhaps opinion leaders do not change their most basic foreign policy orientations until individuals within their ranks articulate and disseminate new compelling rationales for doing so. In other words, the process of individual belief change among leaders—like that of the mass public—may be related to the wider public debate (Zaller 1992).

7. "A *value*," as defined by Rokeach (1973, 5), "is an enduring belief that a specific mode of conduct or end state of existence is personally or socially preferable to an opposite or converse mode of conduct or end-state of existence." Kinder and Sears (1985, 674) refer to values as "general and enduring standards."

Typically, values are thought to hold "a more central position than attitudes" within "one's . . . cognitive system" (Rokeach 1973, 18; see also Kinder and

Sears 1985, 674) and to "lead us to take particular positions on social issues" as well as "predispose us to favor one particular political or religious ideology over another" (Rokeach 1973, 13). See also Rokeach [1968] 1972, 159–60.

8. McClosky and Zaller demonstrate that the widely held American values associated with democracy and capitalism are in tension with each other and that this tension is reflected in the split between "liberalism" and "conservatism." To some extent both sets of values are embraced by virtually all American leaders, but the stronger adherents of democratic values call themselves liberals, while the stronger adherents of capitalist values call themselves conservatives.

9. Wittkopf explicitly argues that these dimensions are orthogonal:

> Because the two internationalism dimensions are independent statistically . . . it is not possible to know an individual's position on one dimension by knowing his or her position on the other; only by considering the two together is it possible to appropriately describe an individual's foreign policy beliefs. (1986, 428)

However, Holsti and Rosenau (1990, 100) find in their Foreign Policy Leadership Project (FPLP) data that "there was a tendency for persons expressing negative views to a CI item to react positively toward MI questions, and vice versa."

10. Using principal components analysis, I will demonstrate that the first factor in the unrotated solution—that factor that explains the largest amount of variance in the data—can be characterized as a liberalism/conservatism dimension, regardless of whether the questions employed are about foreign or domestic policy. This is not to say that leaders' beliefs are unidimensional or that the liberalism/conservatism dimension captures the full complexity of their beliefs; only that the left-to-right continuum remains an important and useful predictor of leaders' foreign policy opinions.

11. I borrowed this phrase from Holsti and Rosenau (1984, 181).

Chapter 2

1. The interviews cited in this chapter were conducted between May and August of 1991. I conducted fourteen interviews during that period with officials from the State Department, the National Security Council (NSC), and within the intelligence community.

2. For instance, Tetlock wrote in 1983:

> The seemingly unresolvable (now thirty-seven years old) debate over American nuclear policy toward the Soviet Union illustrates the profound effects of images on foreign policy thinking. Two rival images have dominated the debate: What I shall call the deterrence (hard-line) and conflict spiral (soft-line) images. . . . These images rest on fundamentally different

assumptions concerning the nature of American-Soviet relations . . . and the types of policies most likely to guarantee stability and peace. (69–70)

3. Holsti and Rosenau used this latter label before the Cold War actually ended. For instance, they use the term in their 1984 book *American Leadership in World Affairs*.

4. The third belief cluster that Holsti and Rosenau identified, "Semi-Isolationists," counseled limited involvement in world problems.

5. For a more nuanced account of this political struggle, especially during the Reagan administration, see Dallin and Lapidus 1983. They divide political elites into three groups: an "essentialist" approach—similar to the hard-line view discussed here—which "defines the Soviet system as inherently evil, sees little prospect for change, and denies the benefits of piecemeal accommodation" (1983, 206) and an "interactionist" approach—similar to the soft-line position discussed here—which "involves greater recognition of differences, even uncertainties, within the Soviet elite. . . . assumes a learning process that includes significant feedback from Soviet experience abroad. . . . and generally assumes a more pervasive interdependence between the two adversary systems" (1983, 206). The authors add another category, the "mechanistic" approach, which "is concerned with Soviet behavior, not essences. It views the Soviet threat as primarily geopolitical and takes the traditional view that power can and must be checked with equal or superior power" (1983, 206).

6. The Executive Committee of the Committee on the Present Danger (CPD), for instance, included such well-known names as Dean Rusk, former secretary of state; Eugene Rostow, former undersecretary of state; Paul Nitze, former deputy secretary of defense; William Colby, former director of central intelligence; Richard Pipes, professor of Russian history at Harvard University; Lane Kirkland, secretary-treasurer of the AFL-CIO; Norman Podhoretz, editor of *Commentary;* Elmo Zumwalt, former chief of naval operations; Andrew Goodpaster, former NATO Supreme Allied Commander, Europe; Richard Scaife, publisher of the *Tribune Review;* and many more. See Sanders 1983, 154–60.

7. For a discussion of the attack on the policy of détente, see Sanders 1983a, 1983b; Barnet 1981; Dalby 1990; Garthoff 1985; Caldwell 1991.

8. During the subsequent confirmation hearings, the

> CPD Executive Committee and Board Members testified on 17 different occasions before the Senate Foreign Relations and Armed Services Committee . . . participated in 479 TV and radio programs, press conferences, debates and public forums on SALT and the military balance; and distributed over 200,000 copies of Committee pamphlets and reports, including eleven updatings of Nitze's attacks on SALT II.

This is a quotation from Eugene Rostow at the CPD's 1979 annual meeting (see Sanders 1983b, 13).

9. Holsti and Rosenau (1986) found that the three belief clusters they had

identified in 1976 persisted into the 1980s. More specifically, they found the same belief clusters in their 1980 and 1984 samples. In other words, although the hard-line perspective gained dominance in the political debate in the early 1980s, the basic cleavage among opinion leaders persisted until at least 1984.

10. As Sanders (1983b, 18) writes, the committee had reason to gloat on election day. After all, it

> had placed forty-six of its members on Reagan's advisory task force and was about to garner over thirty high-level positions (fifty if one counts those serving in a part-time capacity) in the new Administration. The CPD now had the golden opportunity to put into practice the policies preached since its founding. The fortunes of Reagan's foreign policy in the years ahead would prove to be as closely tied to the CPD as his candidacy had been a referendum on the Committee's views.

11. According to Lemann (1984, 73) "defense spending . . . increased 80.2 percent in what are called 'nominal' dollars—that is, dollars not adjusted for inflation—and 48.7 percent in constant dollars" during Reagan's first term.

12. As David Gergen, then White House communications director, later acknowledged, "Zero Option said we *won't* deploy if you take yours out. They clearly weren't going to accept that" (Hertsgaard 1988, 273; emphasis in original). Likewise, the initial START proposal in 1982 called for the Soviet Union to reduce its ICBM warheads by 60 percent in exchange for limitations on the number of future weapons the United States would deploy (Mandelbaum and Talbott 1987, 122). This proposal was also considered to be "non-negotiable" by senior White House officials (Hertsgaard 1988, 279). For a detailed account of arms control efforts in the early Reagan administration, see Talbott 1984.

13. Indeed, individuals would be expected to incorporate new information about the Soviet Union in a manner that would reinforce their previous "images" of that country.

14. For a more detailed account of this period, see Oberdorfer 1991 and Garthoff 1994.

15. Garthoff (1994, 769–70) writes, "In retrospect, it is clear that the single most significant factor not only in turning American-Soviet relations back from confrontation to détente and even beyond during the decade of the 1980s was the impact of Mikhail Gorbachev. Given the policies pursued by Reagan and later Bush, without Gorbachev American-Soviet relations throughout the 1980s and into the 1990s would almost certainly have continued on the same basic course as they did in 1984–85, with minor variations in a pattern of continuing competition." Many conservative analysts, of course, offered a different interpretation, attributing credit to the policies of Ronald Reagan. See Deudney and Ikenberry (1992) and Kinsley (1989) for a discussion of this debate. See also Gaddis (1989) and MccGwire (1995).

16. As will become clear, not all analysts interpreted Gorbachev's actions in this way.

17. Secretary of State George Shultz (1993, 760) recalls that the American team was "surprised" after the initial session between Reagan and Gorbachev at Reykjavik: "Gorbachev's proposals were heading dramatically in our direction. He was laying gifts at our feet—or, more accurately, on the table—concession after concession."

18. Reagan had sent an earlier version of this proposal in a letter to Gorbachev dated July 25, 1986. At that time, Caspar Weinberger, the secretary of defense, Admiral William Crowe, chairman of the Joint Chiefs of Staff (JCS), and others had been convinced that the proposal would be rejected by the Soviets. After all, the Soviet Union relied much more heavily on ballistic missiles than the United States, while the United States had an advantage in bombers and cruise missiles. See Oberdorfer (1991, 174) and Garthoff (1994, 279).

19. The U.S. position, as written down, offered to eliminate ballistic missiles. But Reagan verbally agreed to the elimination of all nuclear weapons. See Shultz (1993, 768–73) and Adelman (1989, 80–82).

20. Interview by author with a high-level intelligence official, July 1991. Leaders within the intelligence community were equally skeptical about Soviet intentions to leave Afghanistan. They thought that Soviet hints about withdrawal were political deception, and they were surprised when the troops started to leave. Oberdorfer (1991, 274) provides a telling illustration of the depth of their skepticism. He reports that Michael Armacost, then undersecretary of state, "who had special responsibility for policy regarding Afghanistan," had come to believe by the early weeks of 1988 that the Soviets "were preparing to withdraw." But Robert Gates, then deputy director of the CIA, bet Armacost $25 that he was wrong, and Fritz Ermarth, then the CIA national intelligence officer for the Soviet Union, bet him $50.

21. For a description of Van Cleave, see Lemann 1984.

22. For a detailed account of how relaxation in the tension between the superpowers affected the 1988 election, see Blumenthal 1990.

23. Bush reportedly warned Gorbachev privately that he "would have to do and say many things" during the 1988 campaign to prove to Reagan supporters that he was not a "closet liberal" and that the Soviet leader should not be offended. See Beschloss and Talbott 1993, 3–4.

24. For a similar analysis of mass opinion, see Yankelovich and Smoke 1988.

25. Interview by author with a State Department official, June 1991. The Bush appointees were a close-knit group with a common past. Bush had served as the director of the CIA under the Ford administration. James Baker, the secretary of state, had been Ford's campaign advisor during the 1976 presidential election. Brent Scowcroft, the national security advisor, had held that same position under Ford, replacing Kissinger when he moved over to State. Dick Cheney, the secretary of defense, had been Ford's chief of staff. And Lawrence Eagleburger, the deputy secretary of state, and Scowcroft had both worked at Kissinger's consulting firm before their appointments.

26. Interview by author with a State Department official, June 1991. The Bush appointees were skeptical about Gorbachev, some political analysts suggested,

because they had observed the backlash against the policy of détente during the 1970s. David Gergen, a political commentator and a former director of communications during the Reagan administration, wrote:

> Cheney and Scowcroft were both at the Ford White House when détente crumbled as the Soviets built up both their military and their empire. . . . And Baker has vivid memories of a conservative Ronald Reagan almost pushing Ford aside for the Republican nomination by attacking détente so sharply that Ford had to drop the word—and almost had to drop Kissinger.

See David Gergen 1989, C2.

27. Throughout his career, Gates had been vehemently anti-Soviet. He had served at the CIA between 1981 and 1988, first as special assistant to then Director William Casey, and then as deputy director of intelligence. During that tenure, according to analysts from the CIA Office of Soviet Analysis (SOVA), he slanted intelligence reports to suit his own pessimistic views of the Kremlin or to cater to such views as held by William Casey and he suppressed dissenting points of view. See U.S. Congress 1991.

28. Gates accompanied Baker to a meeting with Gorbachev in 1989. Gorbachev is reported to have commented upon meeting Gates that "I understand that the White House has a special cell assigned to the task of discrediting Gorbachev. And I've heard that you are in charge, Mr. Gates." He then turned to Baker and joked, "Perhaps if we are able to work out our problems, Mr. Gates will be out of a job" (Beschloss and Talbott 1993, 66).

29. Interview by author with a high-level intelligence official, July 1991.

30. Interview by author with a State Department official, May 1991.

31. I learned in interviews with State Department officials that the Policy Planning Staff shared this "less skeptical" view of Gorbachev.

32. Kennan's declaration that the Soviet Union, once motivated by an ideological fervor to seek world domination, had been transformed into a great power with normal aspirations was reprinted on the op-ed page of the *New York Times*. See Kennan 1989.

33. Veteran political journalist James Reston articulated the growing sentiment in Washington with particular flair:

> In politics as in love, there's a time when you have to kiss the girl. I think that this time is one of those times in history, and we're holding back. I feel in my guts that it's wrong—that this is a moment when we should do more than be prudent and cautious.

See Apple Jr. 1989, L34.

34. Interview by author with a State Department official, June 1991.

35. When Scowcroft reviewed one of these speeches, he wrote "very euphoric" in the margin (see Friedman 1989b, A10).

36. This is not to say, however, that Gorbachev had foreseen the extent or

pace of changes that he would unleash. Most likely, Gorbachev expected re-formed communist governments to stay in power and, certainly, East Germany to remain an independent country. As a White House foreign policy aide told reporter Don Oberdorfer, "The Soviets thought they were creating lots of little Gorbachevs . . . so did we." See Oberdorfer 1991, 355.

37. Interview by author with a high-level intelligence official, July 1991.

38. The Bush administration deserves credit for its handling of the reunifica-tion of Germany. Despite the Soviet Union's weak position, the administration avoided acting triumphant. Their goal was to anchor a reunified Germany within the framework of NATO—obviously a position that would be difficult for the Soviets to agree to. The Soviets, for obvious reasons, preferred that Germany remain neutral. The State Department, and especially the Policy Planning Staff, devised the two-plus-four framework. Their strategy was "to find a way to make the Soviets not feel threatened." In Baker's words, the administration tried to provide Gorbachev with "cover" against his domestic critics. This policy was initially controversial. According to one State Department official, there were some within the administration, such as Robert Blackwill at the National Secu-rity Council (NSC), who thought that the Soviets would interfere with the reunifi-cation process, that "history was on our side," and that the West should "cram an agreement down the Soviets' throat." Interview by author with a State De-partment official, June 1991.

39. Garthoff (1994, 408) points to one particular incident to illustrate how much the changes in Europe had affected American thinking about the Soviet Union. In December 1989, Secretary of State James Baker said that the United States would not object if the Soviet Union felt it necessary to intervene in Romania to prevent bloodshed or defeat for the reformers. While noting the questionable merit of this suggestion, Garthoff observes that it "was a remark-able reflection of a basic shift in outlook toward seeing the Soviet Union as a force contributing to positive change in the world rather than assuming it to be a permanent source of destabilization and threat. It would have been hard to find a more striking example reflecting American recognition of the end of the Cold War."

40. Webster's analysis was reinforced by a CIA/DIA annual report presented to the Joint Economic Committee the following month. The report concluded that "Moscow continues to reduce and restructure its forces, the economic ur-gency of reducing the burden of defense shows no sign of abating" and that "the Soviet leadership is trying to free up resources for the domestic economy by cutting its cost of empire" (U.S. Congress 1990b, 43, 46).

Senator Daniel P. Moynihan, Democrat of New York, argued that the CIA had overestimated the size of the Soviet economy and therefore its military threat. This distorted view of the Soviets, Moynihan asserted, may have led to the country's spending a fortune in defense during the Reagan presidency. See Wines 1990c, A6.

41. The 1990 CCFR survey was administered in October and November of that year.

42. In the 1994 CCFR elite poll, after changes in the U.S. troop levels within Europe had already been made, 6 percent wanted to increase commitment to NATO, 57 percent wanted to keep the commitment where it was, and 37 percent wanted to decrease our commitment or withdraw completely. Likewise, when asked about defense spending in 1994—again after substantial cuts had already been made in U.S. budgets—16 percent wanted to expand spending, 50 percent wanted to keep it the same, and 33 percent wanted to decrease it. See Rielly 1995.

43. See, for example, John Felton 1990.

44. Director George Kolt and his two deputies, Grey Hodnett and Steve Kaplan, pushed the position that the United States should distance itself from Gorbachev and initiate contact with Boris Yeltsin or other democratic leaders. At one point, Scowcroft, hinting that SOVA was overstepping its bounds by suggesting policy rather than providing analysis, said to William Webster, "Why doesn't George Kolt just make it simple and go work for Yeltsin?" (Beschloss and Talbott 1993, 349). Analysts within SOVA were also discontent with the "politicization" of the leadership of the organization. A ballad, written by an anonymous author, was produced in May 1991 and widely disseminated. The second half included the passage "SOVA makes her living now by lying on her back. Her golden gown integrity lays tattered, torn, and limp; Poor SOVA is a prostitute and Georgie [Kolt] is her pimp." A copy of this ballad was given to me by an administration official.

45. Interview by author with David Trachenberg, CPD, August 1991.

46. The organization had folded by August 1992.

47. Although the LOP panel study has 660 respondents, only those who answered the question in both years are included in the turnover tables.

Chapter 3

1. For an excellent review of this literature, see Holsti 1992.

2. For instance, Bardes and Oldendick (1978) and Chittick and Billingsley (1989) reported five factors whereas Mandelbaum and Schneider (1979) and Wittkopf (1990) reported two. However, this discrepancy is partly an artifact of the nature and number of the questions used in the factor analyses and whether or not individual question items were grouped into scales.

3. Their results were not entirely clear-cut. The goals that loaded high on the cooperative factor included "keeping peace in the world"; "securing adequate supplies of energy"; "fostering international cooperation to solve common problems, such as food, inflation, and energy"; "worldwide arms control"; "helping solve world inflation"; "combatting world hunger"; "maintaining a balance of power among nations"; "strengthening the United Nations"; and "helping to improve the standard of living in less developed countries." The goals that loaded high on the militaristic or interventionist factor were "containing communism"; "protecting the interests of American business abroad"; "strengthening countries who are friendly toward us"; "defending our allies' security"; "protect-

ing weaker nations against foreign aggression"; "helping to bring a democratic form of government to other nations"; and "promoting the development of capitalism abroad."

4. In an earlier analysis, Bardes and Oldendick (1978, 499–502) factor analyzed thirty-three questions from the 1974 CCFR data on the mass public and found the following five factors: (1) *militarism* "is solely concerned with militaristic strategies for preserving world order"; (2) *involvement* "describes the degree to which the United States should be involved in world affairs"; (3) the *world problems* factor "is defined by questions suggesting that solving worldwide problems such as inflation, hunger, arms control and improving the standard of living are important goals for U.S. foreign policy"; (4) *détente* is defined by variables that "emphasize the need to exist with allies and enemies"; (5) the last factor "reflects an explicit dimension of support for the United Nations and other international organizations." Note, however, that the first three factors, at least, could be conceptualized within Mandelbaum and Schneider's framework.

5. Even though Holsti and Rosenau's methods are somewhat different, I included them within the "factor analytic approach" because their work overlaps with this body of literature.

6. With cross-sectional data, the only way to measure people's past beliefs is to ask them to recall those beliefs. People's recollections, of course, are of questionable reliability. For the differences between sequential cross-sectional studies and panel studies, see appendix B.

The seven groups were as follows: "Supporters" favored "complete military victory" throughout the war; "Converted Supporters" had not favored this goal at the start of the war but did so by the end; "Ambivalent Supporters" favored "complete military victory" at the start of the war but then became ambivalent; "Ambivalents" took the middle ground throughout the war; "Ambivalent Critics" had favored "complete withdrawal" but then moved to an ambivalent position; "Converted Critics" had supported "complete military victory" at the start of the war but favored "complete withdrawal" by the end; "Critics" had favored "complete withdrawal" throughout the war.

7. Chittick and Billingsley conducted their own elite survey, factor analyzed similar questions and found five factors—three of which corresponded to Holsti and Rosenau's belief types. They labeled the first factor "Post–Cold War Internationalists": issues such as "strengthening the UN," "worldwide arms control," "protecting the global environment," "promoting and defending human rights," "combatting world hunger," and "providing asylum for refugees from war torn countries" loaded highly on this factor. They labeled the second factor "Cold War Internationalists": issues such as "providing military aid to Third World countries," "matching Soviet military strength," "strengthening local police forces in unstable countries," and "preventing Soviet expansion into Third World countries" loaded highly on this factor. The fourth factor, labeled "Semi-Isolationists" was defined by questions such as "dealing effectively with U.S. domestic problems," "setting a good example for other countries to follow," and

"keeping American industry competitive." Note that the first two factors sound remarkably like the cooperative and interventionist factors identified by Mandel-baum and Schneider.

Wittkopf (1986, 430–31) speculated that the "Cold War Internationalists" and "Post–Cold War Internationalists" were "not two unrelated belief systems but . . . instead the opposite ends of a single dimension—the head and the tail of a single bird." He also conceived of the "Semi-Isolationists" as occupying one end of a dimension that had internationalists on the other.

8. He employed many more survey questions than prior analyses, over more years, and analyzed both mass and elite data. One major difference with his methodological approach, however, was that he combined questions into seven scales and then used exploratory factor analysis on the scales themselves.

9. Past scholarship, according the Wittkopf (1986, 436), had failed to "incor-porate the antithesis of isolationism" in their analyses: they had missed the internationalist belief type.

10. However, they note in a footnote that "Factor analyses of the 1976, 1980, and 1984 data confirmed that MI and CI were consistently the most important factors, and the items selected to represent MI and CI had consistently high loadings" (98).

11. They noted that the MI dimension was defined by "two core elements: attitudes toward communism and the use of force" (98). They used the following seven question items to measure it: (1) "There is considerable validity in the 'domino theory' that when one nation falls to communism, others nearby will follow a similar path"; (2) "Any communist victory is a defeat for America's national interest"; (3) "The Soviet Union is generally expansionist rather than defensive in its foreign policy goals"; (4) "There is nothing wrong with using the C.I.A. to try to undermine hostile governments"; (5) "The United States should take all steps including the use of force to prevent the spread of communism"; (6) "Containing communism" as a foreign policy goal; and (7) "It is not in our interest to have better relations with the Soviet Union because we are getting less than we are giving to them."

The "essential elements" of the CI dimension were "attitudes toward détente and active cooperation with other nations" (100). They used the following items to measure it: (1) "It is vital to enlist the cooperation of the UN in settling international disputes"; (2) "The United States should give economic aid to poorer countries even if it means higher prices at home"; (3) "Helping to improve the standard of living of less developed countries" as a foreign policy goal; (4) "Worldwide arms control" as a foreign policy goal; (5) "Combatting world hunger" as a foreign policy goal; (6) "Strengthening the United Nations" as a foreign policy goal; and (7) "Fostering international cooperation to solve common problems, such as food, inflation, and energy" as a foreign policy goal.

12. Four question items were changed (see previous endnote for original wording of questions). On the question about the domino theory, they changed the word "communism" to "aggressor nations" on the 1992 questionnaire. Like-

wise, on the question about whether the Soviet Union is expansionist, they now used the word "Russia." On the question about whether the United States should use force to "prevent the spread of communism," they used the phrase "to prevent aggression by any expansionist power." Finally, they dropped the question about whether it is in "our interest to have better relations with the Soviet Union" and added "Rather than simply countering our opponent's thrusts, it is necessary to strike at the heart of the opponent's power."

13. Americans' images of the Soviet Union, he speculates, may even precede the development of basic foreign policy objectives:

> If leaders see the U.S.S.R. as defensive and conservative, they may think that it is safe to emphasize goals like human rights in Third World clients or to put more energy into combatting hunger. Leaders who see a great threat may stress containment and grant only secondary importance to other worthy objectives. (1986, 845)

While Herrmann raises the question of whether leaders' broader postures toward international affairs are derived from their perceptions about the Soviet Union, he considered the issue beyond the scope of his data.

14. Herrmann qualified his conclusions regarding the extent to which leaders' images about the Soviet Union organize diverse foreign policy attitudes into an integrated belief system. On the one hand, he found that "It is possible to predict a good many policy choices from a global schema" (869), that is, from respondents' perceptions about the Soviet Union. Yet, "there are differences across regions" (869). In particular, the Soviet-containment index was only weakly associated with policy issues related to the Middle East. He therefore proposed that future research "might profitably move . . . toward disaggregating 'belief systems' into general and more situational perceptions with models that consider different combinations of schemata" (869).

15. In their view, Americans used their images of the Soviet Union as a heuristic. People latched "onto the most salient feature of the international environment"—the main U.S. adversary—and developed "prescriptive beliefs from their perceptions of this feature" (1990, 4).

16. Hurwitz and Peffley also found "evidence of impressive stability in respondents' images of the Soviet Union" (453). This finding is not surprising considering the timing of their study: even the second wave predates the series of events, beginning with the demolition of the Berlin Wall, that finally ended the Cold War.

Bartels (1994) makes a distinction between how the informed public and the uninformed public reacted to changes in the Soviet Union. Analyzing the 1992 and earlier National Election Studies (NES) data, Bartels argues that "changing perceptions of the Soviet Union" among the less-informed population "were apparently not sufficient to precipitate significant restructuring of related policy preferences, even for the rather proximate issues of containing communism and defense spending" (497–98). Only "the informed stratum of the general public has so far succeeded in grasping . . . the implications for U.S. defense policy of the declining Soviet threat" (498).

17. As noted earlier, Wittkopf is an exception: he applies factor analysis to various indexes rather than to individual questions.

18. Bardes and Oldendick (1978), Mandelbaum and Schneider (1979), and Wittkopf (1990) all use the CCFR data but use different years and different questions (see also Herrmann 1986, 852). Chittick and Billingsley (1989) and Holsti and Rosenau (1990, 98) each administered their own elite surveys.

19. Indeed, as noted earlier, a similar cleavage was described by Holsti and Rosenau (1984), who were using a different technique for analyzing their data: they portrayed one belief type as placing priority on diplomacy and cooperation (and aiding poorer countries) and another belief type as placing priority on exhibitions of strength and resolve (and protecting ourselves and our allies from the Soviet threat).

20. There may be other postures as well.

21. There are some differences. As noted earlier, Bardes and Oldendick find that questions about détente and international organizations load on separate factors, whereas Wittkopf and Holsti and Rosenau consider these issues to be an aspect of CI.

22. When Holsti and Rosenau (1990) first applied Wittkopf's MI/CI scheme to their own data, they created an MI measure with seven questions—six of which had a direct reference to the Soviet Union or to the containment of communism. In their more recent work, Holsti and Rosenau (1993) updated some of their old questions to use in the 1992 MI scale: they replaced references to communism with phrases such as "aggressor nations" or "expansionist power." But out of seven questions in their 1992 MI scale, two items still mentioned communism and one mentioned the "expansionist nature" of Russia; the other four were about the use of military power more generally. See previous endnotes for more information about these changes in question wording.

23. The two dimensions may not in fact be orthogonal. When Holsti and Rosenau (1990, 100) measure them using elite data, they find "a tendency for persons expressing negative views to a CI item to react positively toward MI questions, and vice versa." I replicated their scales, using the exact question wordings, for the 1988 LOP respondents. (Remember that these 1988 LOP respondents are a subgroup of the 1988 FPLP sample.) I found that the MI and CI scales were substantially correlated with each other ($r = .51$). Also, Mandelbaum and Schneider (1979, 42) find a slight positive association between the factors ($r = .29$) using mass data.

24. For instance, Holsti and Rosenau (1988, 274) find that "The hardliners and, to a lesser extent, the internationalists . . . tend to be domestic conservatives, whereas accommodationists are predominantly liberal on domestic policy." Holsti (1994) also considers how domestic belief types (that is, "liberals," "populists," "libertarians," and "conservatives") answer foreign policy questions and how belief types from each policy domain overlap with ideological self-identification and party identification.

25. By genuine attitude change, I mean that the respondents held firm beliefs, properly recorded, at time 1, and firm beliefs, properly recorded, at time 2, but those beliefs are different (Putnam, Leonardi, and Nanetti 1979, 469).

26. Philip Converse (1964) attributed the instability in mass beliefs over time to the measurement of "nonattitudes." He reported the results of a panel study on the American electorate conducted by the University of Michigan Research Center: the correlations over time between the respondents' views on particular political issues in 1958 and just two years later, in 1960, were quite low. To explain such instability, Converse (1964, 243) posited that the "mass public contains significant proportions of people who, for lack of information about a particular dimension of controversy, offer meaningless opinions that vary randomly in direction during repeated trials over time."

Achen, in response to Converse, argued that the instability in mass beliefs is due to the inadequacy of the measurement instrument rather than to the "vague minds" of typical American citizens. "If survey questions are vague," Achen argued, "then even perfectly stable respondents will appear to be inconsistent" (Achen 1975, 1221). Using the same data set as Converse, Achen developed a model for estimating the measurement error variance that can be used when there are three waves of panel data. With this model, he concluded that attitudes in the mass public were much more stable than Converse had surmised. By this account, instability in respondents' opinion choice is due to vague question wording, coding error, and so on.

27. It is not my purpose here to address the debate about measurement error in survey data.

28. It should be noted that Converse (1964) reported correlations over time (tau beta) for various issues—such as federal housing, foreign military aid, foreign economic aid, federal aid to education, isolationism, and guaranteed employment—that were all less than .4 in a 1958–60 panel study. He concluded that these correlations were evidence of attitude instability. Only two correlations were notably higher: the correlation for school desegregation (still less than .5) and for party identification (the highest at .7).

29. Converse's logic was as follows. Elites display greater "static constraint" between attitudes because their beliefs are more crystallized and better organized. It follows, then, that their attitudes would remain stable over time.

30. When Achen reevaluated the same mass panel study that Converse had used according to respondent background variables, he concluded that

> The well-informed and the interested have nearly as much difficulty with the questions as does the ordinary man. *Measurement error is primarily a fault of the instruments, not of the respondents.* (1975, 1229; emphasis in original)

Another implication of Achen's argument is that the observed correlations underrepresent the stability of attitudes over time.

31. For instance, the interwave correlation on the issue of defense spending

was .36 for the 1972–76 National Election Studies (NES) panel, whereas it was .62 and .80 for the 1980–84 and 1984–88 delegate panel studies, respectively. The other two issue items that were comparable across samples included abortion and busing. The correlation for the mass sample on abortion was .62 compared to .75 and .82 for the elite samples. On busing, the respective correlations were .53 for the mass sample and .79 and .80 for the elite samples.

One might contest that the time period for the mass and elite sample is different and that this would affect the results. However, Jennings also supplies data for an 1972–80 elite panel study. That study shares questions about social groups and sentiments toward public figures with the 1972–76 mass panel study. And, again, the stability over time for the elite sample is consistently higher. See Jennings 1992, 440.

32. Other studies exist but have small sample sizes or were administered over short time periods. For instance, Converse and Pierce (1986) report on a 1967–68 panel study of thirty French deputies. Brown (1970), using an American sample of eighteen "political articulates" and eighteen "political inarticulates," found relatively high correlations over time for a period of several weeks and found little difference between the two groups. Madsen and Sheth (1977) argue that nonattitudes are a problem in the elite stratum as well as the mass stratum, marshaling evidence from a panel study of forty local political leaders from the Indian state of Gujarat over a two-month period in 1966.

33. This panel study had a six-year time span between waves. The first wave was administered in 1970 and the second in 1976.

34. The "Left-Right Issues Index" measured ideological orientations. The "Index of Alienation from Pluralist Politics" was "a summary measure based on ten empirically intercorrelated items, concerning such issues as freedom of political propaganda, the trustworthiness of politicians, the divisiveness of parties and pressure groups, the legitimacy of political considerations in policy deliberation, and the appropriateness of strong government, regardless of programmatic considerations" (482).

35. The "Political Elitism Index" measured "attitudes toward participation by ordinary citizens in public affairs" (482).

36. These three sources of comparative data most likely provide a strict or conservative benchmark for attitude stability. First, it is conceivable that the participants from these past elite panel studies were more ideological than the LOP respondents: party delegates are likely a more politicized group than the wide spectrum of influential people who participated in the LOP study; the Italian elites were not only politicians but also lived in a more politicized culture than exists in the United States.

Second, even under normal circumstances, we would expect that respondents' correlations over time would be higher on domestic questions than foreign policy questions (Converse and Markus 1979). This is especially true when the international arena is in flux.

37. We can correct the correlation coefficient for attenuation due to measurement error. As Carmines and Zeller (1979, 48) put it, "if we can estimate the

reliability of each variable, then we can use these estimates to determine what the correlation between the two variables would be if they were made perfectly reliable." We do have estimates of the reliability for each of the measures, the Cronbach alpha. The observed correlation coefficient divided by the square root of the product of the Cronbach alpha scores equals the correlation between the latent variables, that is, the corrected correlation (Carmines and Zeller 1979, 48). In this case the corrected correlation equals 1.00.

38. Surprisingly, however, even this tiny shift in the mean is still statistically significant at the .05 level.

39. The disattenuated correlation coefficient, computed using a formula in Carmines and Zeller (1979, 48), is .97.

40. Indeed, this small shift in attitudes toward greater support for the use of military force may be a response to the successful execution of the Persian Gulf War. That event, in turn, is itself a symbol of the end of the Cold War, as the United States and the Soviet Union fought on the same side.

41. The interwave correlation (for CI88 and CI92), once corrected for random measurement error, equals .86. A word of caution also about interpreting this particular mean-difference score: a look at the individual question items reveals that respondents' attitudes about the United Nations changed between 1988 and 1992 in a liberal direction (toward greater support for the institution), while their attitudes about the other items in the scale changed, only slightly, in a conservative direction (away from providing resources to help these countries). Although all of these question items measure general beliefs about U.S. involvement in international cooperative efforts, it is important to consider what would happen to the CI scales if the question about the United Nations is excised. The answer is that the basic findings do not change: the correlation over time is then .65, and the mean-difference score is .06. In other words, the findings for the reduced CI scales (minus the UN question) do not alter the argument; they still indicate substantial stability in respondents' attitudes toward cooperative internationalism.

42. This observed correlation, once corrected for measurement error, equals .93.

43. To put this mean-difference score in perspective, let us consider the actual change of the mean for the COMM88 and COMM92 indexes as a proportion of the greatest possible change. More precisely, the mean for COMM88 was .55, a score just on the liberal side of the middle of the scale. Once the Soviet Union collapsed, we would expect respondents to move in the liberal direction, or, in other words, toward the position that communism no longer posed a threat. The greatest possible distance, however, that the mean could move between 1988 and 1992 would be from .55 to 1.00—a distance of .45. The actual mean-difference score was .16, or 36 percent of the possible change.

44. Unlike the 1988 data, it is difficult to make a reliable scale to measure leaders' perceptions about Russia in 1992. Without an estimate of the reliability of the 1992 measure, I cannot estimate what the correlation would look like once corrected for measurement error. However, the fact that leaders' different

answers to questions about Russia in 1992 do not intercorrelate highly—and thereby make a reliable scale—is itself an indication of the confusion that leaders felt by the second wave of the panel.

45. If we consider that the mean of SU88 was .41, then the greatest possible distance that the mean could move—if, by 1992, everyone within the sample strongly agreed that Russia posed no future threat to the West—was .59. Although the RUS92 is not, strictly speaking, a comparable scale, it is the best estimate that we have: its mean was .61. Hence, our best estimate of the actual change in the mean is .20, which constituted more than a third (34 percent) of the possible distance.

46. We see the same pattern in other question items. For example, about a third of the sample agreed in 1988 that the Soviet Union was expansionist and also agreed that "there is nothing wrong with using the CIA to try to undermine hostile governments." Of the 196 respondents who had agreed with both statements in 1988, 141 (72 percent) changed their views about the expansionist tendencies of Russia by 1992. Of these 141 respondents, only 39 (28 percent) also changed their views about the CIA, while 102 (72 percent) did not.

Chapter 4

1. Many scholars have taken issue with Converse's depiction of the average citizen as lacking coherent attitudes. For a review of the more general critiques of Converse, see Kinder and Sears 1985; Sniderman and Tetlock 1986.

2. A possible implication of Converse's work was that the mass public was not fit to participate responsibly in governance.

3. Past studies on mass foreign policy beliefs erred, in their view, by attempting to locate the antecedents of foreign policy attitudes using heuristics found to structure domestic preferences, such as "partisanship, social class, and self-interest—which are largely irrelevant to foreign policy considerations. Rather than import domestic constructs into the foreign policy domain, our research has focused on domain-specific heuristics assumed to guide foreign policy decisions among the mass public" (1990, 21).

4. Their theoretical framework—the concept of a schema—suggests a slightly different structure: as they note, it "suggests that attitude structure within a domain is more usefully studied by focusing on the relationship between general and specific attitudes (*vertical* constraint) than by focusing on the relationship between the idea elements at the same level of abstraction (*horizontal* constraint)" (1987, 1100; emphasis in original).

5. Holsti (1994) divides respondents into four belief types according to their answers to domestic policy questions. He uses two crosscutting scales: a person who is liberal on both social and economic issues is classified as a "liberal"; a person liberal on social issues but conservative on economic issues is labeled a "libertarian"; a person conservative on social issues but liberal on economic issues is called a "populist"; and finally, a person conservative on both social and

economic issues is classified as a "conservative." This analysis is similar to an earlier work by Holsti and Rosenau (1988).

6. It is possible that some scholars may have focused on dimensions specific to foreign policy for practical rather than theoretical considerations: the CCFR trend series does not include questions about domestic politics. Also, Holsti and Rosenau (1988, 1990, 1993) probably focus on foreign policy dimensions so as to address and build upon other research findings.

7. A word of caution: due to the collapse of the Soviet Union between panel waves, the scales used to measure leaders' views about the Soviet Union in 1988 and Russia in 1992 are not created from identically worded questions. Without repeated measures, I cannot reject the possibility that these lower correlations are due to the changes in the question wording.

8. For a different view, see Holsti and Rosenau 1980.

9. Equations (1) and (2) may be specified as follows:

$$MI88 = \beta_0 + \beta_1 DOM88 + \beta_2 GENDER + \beta_3 MILSERV \\ + \beta_4 SU88 + \beta_5 WWII + \beta_6 KOREA + \beta_7 VIETNAM + u \tag{1}$$

$$CI88 = \beta_0 + \beta_1 DOM88 + \beta_2 GENDER + \beta_3 MILSERV \\ + \beta_4 SU88 + \beta_5 WWII + \beta_6 KOREA + \beta_7 VIETNAM + u \tag{2}$$

10. Equation (3) may be specified as follows:

$$MI92 = \beta_0 + \beta_1 DOM92 + \beta_2 GENDER + \beta_3 MILSERV \\ + \beta_4 RUS92 + \beta_5 WWII + \beta_6 KOREA + \beta_7 VIETNAM + u \tag{3}$$

11. Equation (4) may be specified as follows:

$$MI92 = \beta_0 + \beta_1 DOM92 + \beta_2 GENDER + \beta_3 MILSERV \\ + \beta_4 RUS92 + \beta_5 WWII + \beta_6 KOREA + \beta_7 VIETNAM + \beta_8 MI88 + u \tag{4}$$

12. Again, two equations were specified (5 and 6), one that includes respondents' past beliefs on this posture and one that does not:

$$CI92 = \beta_0 + \beta_1 DOM92 + \beta_2 GENDER + \beta_3 MILSERV \\ + \beta_4 RUS92 + \beta_5 WWII + \beta_6 KOREA + \beta_7 VIETNAM + u \tag{5}$$

$$CI92 = \beta_0 + \beta_1 DOM92 + \beta_2 GENDER + \beta_3 MILSERV \\ + \beta_4 RUS92 + \beta_5 WWII + \beta_6 KOREA + \beta_7 VIETNAM + \beta_8 CI88 + u \tag{6}$$

13. See also Lumsdaine 1993.

14. I used data from the second wave of the LOP panel. The reader should note, therefore, that the findings were apparent even in the context of a recession.

15. We see this same pattern on other issues. For instance, respondents who support environmental protection at home also believe this is an important issue

to pursue abroad. When asked their opinion about the domestic policy of "relaxing environmental regulation to stimulate economic growth," 486 respondents disagreed in 1992. Of these respondents, 73 percent also considered "protecting the global environment" to be a "very important" foreign policy goal. Among those who supported relaxing environmental regulation at home, only 28 percent believed "protecting the global environment" to be a "very important" foreign policy goal.

16. When asked about redistributing resources to help the poor at home, 94 percent of those elites who identified themselves as "very liberal" agreed, while 96 percent of those who thought of themselves as "very conservative" disagreed (see table 4.12). The same pattern is seen even when the needy reside in another country (table 4.13). When asked about the provision of economic aid to poorer countries, 80 percent of the "very liberal" elites agreed, while 75 percent of the "very conservative" respondents disagreed.

17. As shown in tables 4.14 and 4.15, 83 percent of the "very liberal" respondents and only 2 percent of the "very conservative" agreed with banning the death penalty; 93 percent of the "very conservative" respondents and only 25 percent of the "very liberal" agreed that military force was a necessary international instrument.

18. For an extensive review of liberal and conservative beliefs on foreign policy, see Crabb 1986.

19. I have in mind Gamson and Modigliani's (1966) "Mainstream Model." See also Zaller 1992.

20. This is Converse's (1964, 213) phrase.

21. For a related argument, see Holsti 1994, 26. He writes that

> the *structure* of both domestic and foreign policy beliefs has remained quite stable [between 1984 and 1992]. No doubt one reason for this stability is that both clusters of beliefs appear to be systematically grounded in ideology and partisanship. (Emphasis in original)

Chapter 5

1. As Wittkopf (1990, 166) summarizes this perspective:

> Beginning perhaps as early as 1941, when President Roosevelt secured bipartisan support for the Lend-Lease Act, policymakers, other political elites, and the public at large generally came to support a few fundamental ideas about the ends and often the means of American foreign policy . . . at least until the mid-1960s.

This conventional wisdom is difficult to substantiate with opinion data: there were no elite surveys on foreign policy available.

2. On the benefits of a bipartisan consensus and dangers of dissensus, see, for example, Winik (1989) and Kissinger and Vance (1988). Not everyone agrees

with such analyses. Some authors point out dangers inherent in elite consensus: that it stifles dissent (Falk 1983) or popular participation (Alden and Schurmann 1990).

3. William Schneider (1990, 3002) perceived a different reality: "The Iraq crisis demonstrates that with the end of the Cold War, the political divisions over foreign policy remain the same. The Democrats are the peace party. The Republicans are the strength party."

4. In an unusual take on the subject, Hogan (1992) articulates the position that the entire period following the Second World War was one of agreement on foreign policy. Now that the Cold War is over, he contends, the United States may experience increased ideological and partisan conflict.

5. Tonelson (1993/1994, 4) sees the primary new "fault line" as dividing nationalists and internationalists.

6. The analyses in this chapter (unless otherwise noted) use respondents' ideological self-identification as reported in 1988 to calculate results shown for that year and their ideological self-identification as reported in 1992 to calculate the results for the second wave. The substantive results, however, do not change if respondents' 1988 ideological self-identification is used in calculations for both waves. There was a high level of individual stability on this variable: the correlation over time for ideological self-identification is .86.

Also, for the purposes of simplicity, I only use ideological groups—not partisan groups—in this analysis. Not surprisingly, there is a strong overlap between ideology and partisanship. In the 1988 wave, for instance, 71 percent of Democrats considered themselves to be either "very liberal" or "somewhat liberal," and 76 percent of Republicans identified themselves as "very conservative" or "somewhat conservative."

7. Note that these four questions together constitute the MI scales.

8. This question format is more difficult to interpret because there are three response options—whether a particular goal is "very important," "somewhat important," or "not important at all"—and, not surprisingly, the last category is hardly used. I hold that the differences between the ideological groups fall within the first two response options.

9. On the question about "protecting the international environment," 46 percent of conservatives and 87 percent of liberals chose the "very important" option in 1988; 43 percent of conservatives and 77 percent of liberals chose that option in 1992.

With respect to "worldwide arms control," 51 percent of conservatives and 89 percent of liberals believed that this was a "very important" goal in 1988; 53 percent of conservatives and 79 percent of liberals chose that option in 1992.

10. This was probably only a temporary change in attitudes for conservatives. I expect that subsequent leadership surveys will again indicate that liberals and conservatives are polarized in their views toward the United Nations and other multinational institutions.

11. Respondents' placements on the MI88 scale are even more highly associated than past ideology (IDEO88) with their 1992 beliefs about the impetus of

Soviet reform: those who had supported militant internationalism in the past were more likely than those who had opposed that strategy to believe that Reagan's buildup had forced the Soviets to capitulate ($r = .51$); and they were less likely to believe that a "new generation of Soviet leaders" was responsible for such changes ($r = -.34$).

12. Respondents' past positions toward militant internationalism (MI88) were associated with their 1992 views on this question: the Pearson r was substantial at $-.54$.

13. See, for example, Lewis 1992, A31.

14. See also Krauthammer 1993, 74.

Chapter 6

1. On all these issues respondents' past beliefs were still predictive of their 1992 positions. That is, respondents' positions relative to those of the other respondents remained fairly constant, but there was a sea change in opinion.

Appendix A

1. Much of the discussion here is drawn from an earlier article; see Murray 1992.

2. This method is unusual but not unprecedented. For instance, Gibson (1989), with the cooperation of National Opinion Research Center (NORC), added a second wave onto the 1987 General Social Survey (GSS).

3. They generously allowed me access to their 1988 FPLP sample list and questionnaires.

4. Rosenau (1961, 45) defines opinion makers as "all members of the society who occupy positions which enable them regularly to transmit, either locally or nationally, opinions about any issue to unknown persons outside of their occupational field or about more than one class of issues to unknown professional colleagues."

5. They used several rules of exclusion. "Among those excluded and replaced with the next name were: non-U.S. citizens, persons who failed to list a home address, and professional entertainment and sports figures (many of whom listed only the address of agents)." See Holsti 1990a, 5.

6. They used the following additional sampling frames: *Who's Who in American Women; Who's Who in American Politics; Who's Who in Religion;* the *State Department Directory;* the *Directory of National Unions and Employee Associations;* all authors from *Foreign Affairs, Foreign Policy,* and *International Security* for the previous three years; the membership list of the International Studies Association; the *Congressional Directory* (both for senior military officers and media leaders); the entire class at the National War College; and the *Gale Directory of Publications.*

7. Holsti and Rosenau included a postcard along with the questionnaire.

Once a person had sent the completed questionnaire to one address, he or she was instructed to send the postcard to another address. When the postcard was received, the individual was crossed off the mailing list.

8. I am using the terms confidentiality and anonymity as follows. Confidentiality implies that the researcher may know how individual respondents answered the survey questions but has agreed never to disclose this information to others. Any survey conducted through direct personal interviews necessarily relies upon a guarantee of confidentiality. The guarantee of anonymity, in contrast, imposes a stricter safeguard; it implies that even the researcher does not know who the actual respondents are or how they answered the survey questions.

With respect to researchers knowing and keeping records about whether a particular questionnaire came from a particular person, when Gibson (1989), for instance, added a second wave onto the 1987 GSS, he did not have to identify prior respondents; NORC conducts interviews in person for the GSS and keeps careful records of the individuals involved. NORC administered the second wave for Gibson.

9. It is important to emphasize that a user of the FPLP data would never be able to identify individual respondents. The only exception is that a respondent in the survey might be able to identify him or herself—only if he or she had unique demographic characteristics—but no one else.

10. I thank David Kinsella for doing this work.

11. Again, the individuals had to possess unique demographic characteristics (e.g., age, gender, types of degrees, military service, geographical location, etc.) for the particular subsample from which their names were derived.

12. I also provided postcards that the respondents mailed separately from the completed questionnaire.

13. Because the LOP panel data set is a leadership study, we need not be concerned about selection bias per se: the original FPLP sample was never meant to be an accurate representation of the elite population. The term bias, as used here, refers only to the comparability of the LOP panel with the FPLP original sample.

14. Again, I excluded those military officers and labor officials who were drawn from sampling frames other than *Who's Who in America* from the 1988 data. Also, the panel members' demographics were taken from the 1988 wave.

15. Only 10 percent of the questions were statistically significant at the .10 level. Approximately 190 questions were appropriate for this test.

Appendix B

1. The CCFR has collected both mass and elite survey data every four years since 1974 (see Rielly 1975, 1979, 1983, 1987, 1991, 1995). The FPLP has collected survey data on opinion leaders every four years since 1976 (see Holsti and Rosenau 1984, 1986, 1988, 1990, 1993; Holsti 1990a).

2. This is a paraphrase from Zeisel 1957, 217.

Appendix C

1. The validity of these scales is corroborated by their correlations with an appropriate question that was added to the 1992 questionnaire. I asked respondents whether "It is necessary to use force to stop aggression; economic sanctions are not enough." The Pearson coefficient between the MI88 scale and this question was substantial at .54, as was the association with the MI92 scale at .50.

I also asked respondents in 1992 whether "There is nothing wrong with the United States unilaterally using military force abroad." The coefficient with the MI88 scale was again substantial at .53; for the MI92 scale it was .59.

Bibliography

Achen, C. H. 1975. Mass Political Attitudes and the Survey Response. *American Political Science Review* 69: 1218–31.

Adelman, K. 1989. *The Great Universal Embrace: Arms Summitry—A Skeptic's Account*. New York: Simon and Schuster.

Alden, E. H., and F. Schurmann. 1990. *Why We Need Ideologies in American Foreign Policy: Democratic Politics and World Order*. Berkeley: Institute of International Studies, University of California.

Almond, G. 1950. *The American People and Foreign Policy*. New York: Harcourt, Brace.

Apple, R. W., Jr. 1989. Reston, Retiring at 80, Still Looks Up the Road. *New York Times,* November 5, L34.

Babbie, E. 1990. *Survey Research Methods*. Belmont, CA: Wadsworth.

Bailey, T. A. 1948. *The Man in the Street: The Impact of American Public Opinion on Foreign Policy*. New York: Macmillan.

Baltes, P. B., and J. R. Nesselroade. 1979. History and Rationale of Longitudinal Research. In *Longitudinal Research in the Study of Behavior and Development,* edited by J. R. Nesselroade and P. B. Baltes. New York: Academic.

Bardes, B., and R. Oldendick. 1978. Beyond Internationalism: A Case for Multiple Dimensions in the Structure of Foreign Policy Attitudes. *Social Science Quarterly* 59: 496–508.

Barnet, R. J. 1981. *Real Security: Restoring American Power in a Dangerous Decade*. New York: Simon and Schuster.

———. 1992. A Balance Sheet: Lippmann, Kennan, and the Cold War. In *The End of the Cold War: Its Meaning and Implications,* edited by M. J. Hogan. New York: Cambridge University Press.

Bartels, L. M. 1994. The American Public's Defense Spending Preferences in the Post–Cold War Era. *Public Opinion Quarterly* 58: 479–508.

Bernstein, R. A., and W. W. Anthony. 1974. The ABM Issue in the Senate, 1968–1970: The Importance of Ideology. *American Political Science Review* 68: 1198–1206.

Beschloss, M., and S. Talbott. 1993. *At the Highest Levels: The Inside Story of the End of the Cold War*. Boston: Little, Brown.

Blumenthal, S. 1990. *Pledging Allegiance: The Last Campaign of the Cold War*. New York: HarperCollins.

Brandes, L. 1994. *Public Opinion, International Security Policy, and Gender: United States and Great Britain since 1945*. Ph.D. diss., Yale University.

Brown, S. R. 1970. Consistency and the Persistence of Ideology: Some Experimental Results. *Public Opinion Quarterly* 34: 60–68.

Bush, G. 1989. Remarks at the Texas A & M University Commencement Ceremony in College Station, Texas, May 12, 1989. *Weekly Compilation of Presidential Documents* 25 (May 22): 699–702.

Caldwell, D. 1991. *The Dynamics of Domestic Politics and Arms Control: The SALT II Treaty Ratification Debate*. Columbia: University of South Carolina Press.

Carmines, E. G., and R. A. Zeller. 1979. *Reliability and Validity Assessment*. Sage University Paper Series on Quantitative Applications in the Social Sciences, No. 07–017. Beverly Hills: Sage Publications.

Carter, J. 1977. University of Notre Dame: The President's Address at Commencement Exercises at the University. May 22. *Weekly Compilation of Presidential Documents* 13 (May 30): 773–79.

———. 1980. Soviet Military Intervention in Afghanistan. Actions to be Taken by the U.S. January 4. *Vital Speeches of the Day* 46 (January 15): 194–95.

Caute, D. 1978. *The Great Fear: The Anti-Communist Purge under Truman and Eisenhower*. New York: Simon and Schuster.

Campbell, A., P. Converse, W. E. Miller, and D. E. Stokes. [1960] 1980. *The American Voter*. Chicago: University of Chicago Press.

Chace, J. 1978. Is a Foreign Policy Consensus Possible? *Foreign Affairs* 57: 1–16.

Chittick, W. O., and K. R. Billingsley. 1989. The Structure of Elite Foreign Policy Beliefs. *Western Political Quarterly* 42: 201–24.

Congressional Quarterly Almanac. 1988a. Text of 1988 Democratic Party Platform, 87A–90A.

———. 1988b. Republican Party Issues Detailed, Long Platform, 46A–75A.

Converse, P. E. 1964. The Nature of Belief Systems in Mass Publics. In *Ideology and Discontent*, edited by D. E. Apter. New York: Free Press.

Converse, P. E., and G. B. Markus. 1979. Plus ça change . . . : The New CPS Election Study Panel. *American Political Science Review* 73: 32–49.

Converse, P. E., and R. Pierce. 1986. *Political Representation in France*. Cambridge, MA: Harvard University Press, Belknap Press.

Cottam, R. W. 1977. *Foreign Policy Motivation: A General Theory and a Case Study*. Pittsburgh: University of Pittsburgh Press.

Crabb, C. V. 1957. *Bipartisan Foreign Policy: Myth or Reality?* Evanston, IL: Row, Peterson.

———. 1986. *Policy-Makers and Critics: Conflicting Theories of American Foreign Policy*. New York: Praeger.

Crocker, J., S. T. Fiske, and S. E. Taylor. 1984. Schematic Bases of Belief Change. In *Attitudinal Judgement*, edited by J. R. Eiser. New York: Springer-Verlag.

Dalby, S. 1990. *Creating the Second Cold War: The Discourse of Politics*. New York: Guilford Publications.

Dallin, A., and G. W. Lapidus. 1983. Reagan and the Russians: United States Policy toward the Soviet Union and Eastern Europe. In *Eagle Defiant*, edited by K. A. Oye, R. J. Lieber, and D. Rothchild. Boston: Little, Brown.

Davis, J. A. 1985. *The Logic of Causal Order.* Sage University Paper Series on Quantitative Applications in the Social Sciences, No. 07–055. Beverly Hills: Sage Publications.

Destler, I. M., L. H. Gelb, and A. Lake. 1984. *Our Own Worst Enemy: The Unmaking of American Foreign Policy.* New York: Simon and Schuster.

Deudney, D., and G. J. Ikenberry. 1992. Who Won the Cold War? *Foreign Policy* 87: 123–38.

Devroy, A. 1989. Bush and Baker Disclaim Cheney's Gorbachev View. *Washington Post,* May 1, A15.

Etheredge, L. S. 1978. *A World of Men: The Private Sources of American Foreign Policy.* Cambridge, MA: MIT Press.

Falk, R. 1983. Lifting the Curse of Bipartisanship. *World Policy Journal* 1: 127–57.

Felton, J. 1990. Conservatives Poised to Fight Efforts to Slash Defense. *Congressional Quarterly Weekly Report* 28 (January 27): 249–52.

Ferguson, T. 1986. The Right Consensus? Holsti and Rosenau's New Foreign Policy Belief Surveys. *International Studies Quarterly* 30: 411–23.

Ferguson, T., and J. Rogers. 1986. *Right Turn: The Decline of the Democrats and the Future of American Politics.* New York: Hill and Wang.

Fiske, S. T. 1986. Schema-Based versus Piecemeal Politics. In *Political Cognition: The 19th Annual Carnegie Symposium on Cognition,* edited by R. R. Lau and D. O. Sears. Hillsdale, NJ: Lawrence Erlbaum Associates.

Fiske, S., and S. E. Taylor. 1984. *Social Cognition.* New York: Random House.

Fleisher, R. 1985. Economic Benefit, Ideology, and Senate Voting on the B-1 Bomber. *American Politics Quarterly* 13: 200–11.

Friedman, T. 1989a. Senate Leader Asserts U.S. Fails to Encourage Change in East Bloc. *New York Times,* September 19, A1, A14.

———. 1989b. Handling Gorbachev: A Debate among Skeptics. *New York Times,* November 2, A10.

Gaddis, J. L. 1982. *The Strategies of Containment: A Critical Appraisal of Postwar American National Security Policy.* New York: Oxford University Press.

———. 1989. Hanging Tough Paid Off. *Bulletin of Atomic Scientists* (January–February): 11–14.

Gamson, W. A., and A. Modigliani. 1966. Knowledge and Foreign Policy Opinions: Some Models for Consideration. *Public Opinion Quarterly* 30: 187–99.

Garthoff, R. L. 1985. *Détente and Confrontation: American-Soviet Relations from Nixon to Reagan.* Washington, DC: Brookings Institution.

———. 1992. Why Did the Cold War Arise, and Why Did It End? In *The End of the Cold War: Its Meaning and Implications,* edited by M. J. Hogan. New York: Cambridge University Press.

———. 1994. *The Great Transition: American-Soviet Relations and the End of the Cold War.* Washington, DC: Brookings Institution.

Gelb, L. 1992. No More Hawks and Doves. *New York Times,* October 8, A35.

Gergen, D. 1989. Bush's Very Own Ford Foundation: The Cheney-Scowcroft-Baker Team Learned the Same Lessons in the '70s. *Washington Post,* April 2, C2.

Gibson, J. 1989. The Structure of Attitudinal Tolerance in the United States. *British Journal of Political Science* 19: 562–70.

Gorbachev, M. 1988. Excerpts from Speech to U.N. on Major Soviet Military Cuts. *New York Times,* December 8, A16.

Herrmann, R. K. 1985. American Perceptions of Soviet Foreign Policy: Reconsidering Three Competing Perspectives. *Political Psychology* 6: 375–411.

———. 1986. The Power of Perceptions in Foreign-Policy Decision Making: Do Views of the Soviet Union Determine the Policy Choices of American Leaders? *American Journal of Political Science* 30: 841–75.

Hertsgaard, M. 1988. *On Bended Knee: The Press and the Reagan Presidency.* New York: Farrar, Straus, Giroux.

Hinckley, R. H. 1988. Public Attitudes toward Key Foreign Policy Events. *Journal of Conflict Resolution* 32: 295–318.

Hoffman, D. 1989. Gorbachev Seen as Trying to Buy Time for Reform. *Washington Post,* January 23, A9.

———. 1990. The President's New Stand toward Gorbachev: More Wait-and-See. *Washington Post National Weekly Edition,* March 19–25, 11.

Hogan, M. J. 1992. Foreign Policy, Partisan Politics, and the End of the Cold War. In *The End of the Cold War: Its Meaning and Implications,* edited by M. J. Hogan. New York: Cambridge University Press.

Holsti, O. R. 1967. Cognitive Dynamics and Images of the Enemy: Dulles and Russia. In *Enemies in Politics,* edited by D. J. Finlay, O. R. Holsti, and R. R. Fagen. Chicago: Rand McNally.

———. 1988. What Are the Russians Up to Now: The Beliefs of American Leaders about the Soviet Union and Soviet-American Relations, 1976–1984. In *East-West Conflict: Elite Perceptions and Political Options,* edited by M. D. Intriligator and H. Jacobsen. Boulder, CO: Westview.

———. 1990a. *The Domestic and Foreign Policy Beliefs of American Leaders: 1988.* Final Report on National Science Foundation Grant Number SES-87-22646.

———. 1990b. Toward an Operational Definition of Consensus. In *The Domestic and Foreign Policy Beliefs of American Leaders: 1988.* Report to the National Science Foundation on Grant Number SES-87-22646.

———. 1990c. Gender and Political Beliefs of American Leaders, 1976–1988. Paper presented at the annual meeting of the International Studies Association, Washington, D.C.

———. 1991. American Reactions to the U.S.S.R.: Public Opinion. In *Soviet-American Relations after the Cold War,* edited by R. Jervis and S. Bialer. Durham, NC: Duke University Press.

———. 1992. Public Opinion and Foreign Policy: Challenges to the Almond-Lippmann Consensus. *International Studies Quarterly* 36: 439–66.

————. 1994. The Domestic and Foreign Policy Beliefs of American Leaders, during and after the Cold War. Paper presented at the annual meeting of the International Studies Association, Washington, D.C.

Holsti, O. R., and J. N. Rosenau. 1980. Does Where You Stand Depend on When You Were Born? The Impact of Generation on Post-Vietnam Foreign Policy Beliefs. *Public Opinion Quarterly* 44: 1–23.

————. 1984. *American Leadership in World Affairs: Vietnam and the Breakdown of Consensus.* Boston: Allen and Unwin.

————. 1986. Consensus Lost. Consensus Regained?: Foreign Policy Beliefs of American Leaders, 1976–1980. *International Studies Quarterly* 30: 375–409.

————. 1988. The Domestic and Foreign Policy Beliefs of American Leaders. *Journal of Conflict Resolution* 32: 248–94.

————. 1990. The Structure of Foreign Policy Attitudes among American Leaders. *Journal of Politics* 52: 94–125.

————. 1993. The Structure of Foreign Policy Beliefs among American Opinion Leaders—After the Cold War. *Millennium: Journal of International Studies* 22: 235–253.

Hughes, B. B. 1978. *The Domestic Context of American Foreign Policy.* San Francisco: W. H. Freeman.

Hughes, T. L. 1980. The Crack-up: The Price of Collective Irresponsibility. *Foreign Policy* 40: 33–60.

Huntington, S. 1983. The Defense Policy of the Reagan Administration, 1981–1982. In *The Reagan Presidency: An Early Assessment,* edited by Fred Greenstein. Baltimore: Johns Hopkins University Press.

Hurwitz, J., and M. Peffley. 1987. How Are Foreign Policy Attitudes Structured? A Hierarchical Model. *American Political Science Review* 81: 1099–120.

————. 1990. Public Images of the Soviet Union: The Impact on Foreign Policy Attitudes. *Journal of Politics* 52: 3–28.

Ignatius, D. 1989. Why Bob Gates Is the Eeyore of Sovietology. *Washington Post,* May 28, B2.

Jennings, M. K. 1992. Ideological Thinking among Mass Publics and Political Elites. *Public Opinion Quarterly* 56: 419–41.

Jennings, M. K., and R. G. Niemi. 1978. The Persistence of Political Orientations: An Over-Time Analysis of Two Generations. *British Journal of Political Science* 8: 333–63.

Jervis, R. 1976. *Perception and Misperception in International Politics.* Princeton: Princeton University Press.

Kegley, C. W. 1986. Assumptions and Dilemmas in the Study of Americans' Foreign Policy Beliefs: A Caveat. *International Studies Quarterly* 30: 447–71.

Kennan, G. 1989. Just Another Great Power. *New York Times,* April 9, sec. 4, p. 25.

Kennedy, P. M. 1987. *The Rise and Fall of the Great Powers: Economic Change and Military Conflict from 1500 to 2000.* New York: Random House.

Kessler, R. C., and D. F. Greenberg. 1981. *Linear Panel Analysis: Models of Quantitative Change.* New York: Academic.

Key, V. O. 1961. *Public Opinion and American Democracy.* New York: Alfred A. Knopf.

Kim, J., and C. W. Mueller. 1978. *Factor Analysis: Statistical Methods and Practical Issues.* Sage University Paper Series on Quantitative Applications in the Social Sciences, No. 07-014. Beverly Hills: Sage Publications.

Kinder, D. R., and D. O. Sears. 1985. Public Opinion and Political Action. In *Handbook of Social Psychology,* edited by G. Lindzey and E. Aronson. Cambridge, MA: Addison-Wesley.

Kinsley, M. 1989. Who Killed Communism? *New Republic,* December 4, 4.

Kissinger, H. 1987. The Dangers Ahead. *Newsweek,* December 21, 34–41.

Kissinger, H., and C. Vance. 1988. Bipartisan Objectives for American Foreign Policy. *Foreign Affairs* 66 (summer): 899–921.

Koopman, C., J. Snyder, and R. Jervis. 1989. American Elite Views of Relations with the Soviet Union. *Journal of Social Issues* 45: 119–38.

———. 1990. Theory-Driven versus Data-Driven Assessment in a Crisis. *Journal of Conflict Resolution* 34: 694–722.

Krauthammer, C. 1989/1990. Universal Dominion: Toward a Unipolar World. *National Interest* 18: 46–49.

———. 1993. How the Doves Became Hawks. *Time,* May 17, 74.

Kritzer, H. M. 1978. Ideology and American Political Elites. *Public Opinion Quarterly* 42: 484–502.

Lewis, A. 1992. Changing the Rules. *New York Times,* December 4, A31.

Lebow, R., and J. Stein. 1989. The Limits of Cognitive Models: Carter, Afghanistan, and Foreign Policy Change. Mimeograph.

Lemann, N. October 1984. The Peacetime War. *Atlantic Monthly,* 71–94.

Lumsdaine, D. 1992. The Moral Construction of Rationality in International Politics. Paper presented at the annual meeting of the American Political Science Association, Chicago, IL.

———. 1993. *Moral Vision in International Politics: The Foreign Aid Regime, 1949–1989.* Princeton: Princeton University Press.

Madsen, D., and D. L. Sheth. 1977. Non-attitudes among Political Leaders: Some Evidence from a Panel Study. *Political Methodology* 4: 119–37.

Maggiotto, M. A., and E. R. Wittkopf. 1981. American Public Attitudes toward Foreign Policy. *International Studies Quarterly* 25: 601–31.

Mandelbaum, M., and W. Schneider. 1979. The New Internationalisms. In *Eagle Entangled: U.S. Foreign Policy in a Complex World,* edited by K. A. Oye, D. Rothchild, and R. J. Lieber. New York: Longman.

Mandelbaum, M., and S. Talbott. 1987. *Reagan and Gorbachev.* New York: Vintage Books.

May, E. 1973. *"Lessons" of the Past; the Use and Misuse of History in American Foreign Policy.* New York: Oxford University Press.

Maynes, C. W. 1990. America without the Cold War. *Foreign Policy* 78: 3–25.

McClosky, H. 1958. Conservatism and Personality. *American Political Science Review* 52: 27–45.

McClosky, H., and J. Zaller. 1984. *The American Ethos: Public Attitudes toward Capitalism and Democracy.* Cambridge: Harvard University Press.

MccGwire, M. 1995. Generational Change, Not U.S. Bullying, Explains the Gorbachev Revolution. In *Major Problems in American Foreign Relations.* Vol. 2, 4th ed., edited by T. Paterson and D. Merrill. Lexington, MA: D. C. Heath.

Melanson, R. A. 1991. *Reconstructing Consensus: American Foreign Policy since the Vietnam War.* New York: St. Martin's Press.

Menard, S. 1991. *Longitudinal Research.* Sage University Paper Series on Quantitative Applications in the Social Sciences, No. 07–076. Newbury Park, CA: Sage Publications.

Moore, M. 1989. Cheney Predicts Gorbachev Will Fail, Be Replaced. *Washington Post,* April 29, A17.

Moore, M., and P. E. Tyler. 1990. Richard Cheney on the Defensive. *Washington Post Weekly Edition,* April 23–29, 6–7.

Morgenthau, H. [1948] 1993. *Politics among Nations; The Struggle for Power and Peace.* New York: McGraw-Hill.

Moyer, W. 1973. House Voting on Defense: An Ideological Explanation. In *Military Force and American Society,* edited by B. Russett and A. C. Stepan. New York: Harper & Row.

Murray, S. K. 1992. Turning an Elite Cross-sectional Survey into a Panel Study while Protecting Anonymity. *Journal of Conflict Resolution* 36: 586–95.

National Security Council. [1950] 1993. NSC 68: US Objectives and Programs for National Security (April 14, 1950). In *American Cold War Strategy: Interpreting the NSC 68,* edited by E. May. Boston: St. Martin's Press.

New York Times. 1989a. Editorial. George Bush's New World, January 15, E26.

———. 1989b. Editorial. The Cold War Is Over, April 2, E30.

———. 1989c. Editorial. Take Me to Your Leader, May 21, E26.

———. 1989d. Editorial. What East-West Policy?, May 25, A26.

Nixon, R. 1989. American Foreign Policy: The Bush Agenda. *Foreign Affairs* 68: 199–219.

Nunn, S. 1986. The Reykjavik Summit: What Did We Really Agree To? *Congressional Record. Proceedings and Debates of the Ninety-Ninth Congress* 132, (October 17): 33162–64.

Nunnally, J. C. 1978. *Psychometric Theory.* New York: McGraw-Hill.

Oberdorfer, D. 1989a. U.S., Soviets Should Seek 'Points of Mutual Advantage,' Baker Says. *Washington Post,* October 17, A16.

———. 1989b. Baker Blocked Speech by NSC Deputy on Gorbachev Reforms. *Washington Post,* October 28, A18.

———. 1991. *The Turn: From the Cold War to a New Era.* New York: Poseidon Press.

Peffley, M., and J. Hurwitz. 1992. International Events and Foreign Policy Beliefs: Public Response to Changing Soviet-U.S. Relations. *American Journal of Political Science* 36: 431–61.

Putnam, R. D., R. Leonardi, and R. Y. Nanetti. 1979. Attitude Stability among Italian Elites. *American Journal of Political Science* 23: 463–94.

Reagan, R. 1988. National Security Strategy of the United States. *Department of State Bulletin* 88 (April 1988): 1–31.

Reid, T. R. 1988. Dukakis' Soviet Goal: Better Behavior. *Washington Post,* September 14, A4.

Rielly, J. E. 1991b. Public Opinion: The Pulse of the '90s. *Foreign Policy* 82: 79–96.

———. 1995. The Public Mood at Mid-Decade. *Foreign Policy* 98: 76–93.

———, ed. 1975. *American Public Opinion and U.S. Foreign Policy 1975.* Chicago: Chicago Council on Foreign Relations.

———, ed. 1979. *American Public Opinion and U.S. Foreign Policy 1979.* Chicago: Chicago Council on Foreign Relations.

———, ed. 1983. *American Public Opinion and U.S. Foreign Policy 1983.* Chicago: Chicago Council on Foreign Relations.

———, ed. 1987. *American Public Opinion and U.S. Foreign Policy 1987.* Chicago: Chicago Council on Foreign Relations.

———, ed. 1991a. *American Public Opinion and U.S. Foreign Policy 1991.* Chicago: Chicago Council on Foreign Relations.

———, ed. 1995. *American Public Opinion and U.S. Foreign Policy 1995.* Chicago: Chicago Council on Foreign Relations.

Rokeach, M. [1968] 1972. *Beliefs, Attitudes and Values; A Theory of Organization and Change.* San Francisco: Jossey-Bass.

———. 1973. *The Nature of Human Values.* New York: Free Press.

Rosenau, J. N. 1961. *Public Opinion and Foreign Policy: An Operational Formulation.* New York: Random House.

Rosenbaum, D. 1992. Its Red Menace Gone, G.O.P. Platform Re-Aims. *New York Times,* August 13, A21.

Roskin, M. 1974. From Pearl Harbor to Vietnam: Shifting Generational Paradigms and Foreign Policy. *Political Science Quarterly* 89: 563–88.

Russett, B. M. 1970. *What Price Vigilance? The Burdens of National Defense.* New Haven: Yale University Press.

Russett, B. M., and E. C. Hanson. 1975. *Interest and Ideology: The Foreign Policy Beliefs of American Businessmen.* San Francisco: W. H. Freeman.

Russett, B. M., T. Hartley, and S. K. Murray. 1994. The End of the Cold War, Attitude Change, and the Politics of Defense Spending. *PS: Political Science and Politics* 27: 17–21.

Sanders, J. W. 1983a. *Peddlers of Crisis: The Committee on the Present Danger and the Politics of Containment.* Boston: South End.

———. 1983b. *Empire at Bay: Containment Strategies and American Politics at the Crossroads.* New York: World Policy Institute.

———. 1992. The Prospects for 'Democratic Engagement.' *World Policy Journal* 9: 367–87.

Schlesinger, J. 1986. The Dangers of a Nuclear-Free World. *Time,* October 27, 41.

———. 1987. Reykjavik and Revelations: A Turn of the Tide? *Foreign Affairs* 65: 426–46.

Schneider, J. E. 1979. *Ideological Coalitions in Congress.* Westport, CT: Greenwood Press.

Schneider, W. 1990. Persian Gulf Becomes Partisan Issue. *National Journal* (December 8): 3002.

Shultz, G. 1988a. National Success and International Stability in a Time of Change, December 4, 1987. *Department of State Bulletin* 88 (January): 3–7.

———. 1988b. Managing the U.S.-Soviet Relationship. February 5, 1988. *Department of State Bulletin* 88 (April): 38–42.

———. 1993. *Turmoil and Triumph: My Years as Secretary of State.* New York: Charles Scribner's Sons.

Silverstein, B., and C. Flamenbaum. 1989. Biases in the Perception and Cognition of the Actions of Enemies. *Journal of Social Issues* 45: 51–72.

Silverstein, B., and R. R. Holt. 1989. Research on Enemy Images: Present Status and Future Prospects. *Journal of Social Issues* 45: 159–75.

Sniderman, P. M., and P. E. Tetlock. 1986. Interrelationship of Political Ideology and Public Opinion. In *Political Psychology: Contemporary Problems and Issues,* edited by M. G. Hermann. San Francisco: Jossey-Bass.

Spector, P. E. 1992. *Summated Rating Scale Construction: An Introduction.* Sage University Paper Series on Quantitative Applications in the Social Sciences, No. 07–082. Newbury Park, CA: Sage Publications.

Snyder, G. H., and P. Diesing. 1977. *Conflict among Nations: Bargaining, Decision Making, and System Structure in International Crisis.* Princeton: Princeton University Press.

Sulfaro, V. A. 1994. The Influence of Political Sophistication and the Cold War on Foreign Policy Attitudes. Paper presented at the annual meeting of the Midwest Political Science Association, Chicago, IL.

———. 1995. The Influence of Ideology on Congressional Votes. Paper presented at the annual meeting of the Midwest Political Science Association, Chicago, IL.

Talbott, S. 1984. *Deadly Gambits: The Reagan Administration and the Stalemate in Nuclear Arms Control.* New York: Alfred A. Knopf.

Tetlock, P. 1983. Policy-Makers' Images of International Conflict. *Journal of Social Issues* 39: 67–86.

Tonelson, A. 1993/1994. Beyond Left and Right. *National Interest* 34: 3–18.

Tyler, P. E. 1990. Keeping the Threat Alive. *Washington Post Weekly Edition,* February 19–25, 31.

Tyler, P. E., and R. J. Smith. 1989. Study Finds NATO War Plans Outdated. *Washington Post,* November 29, A1.

U.S. Congress. House. 1986. Committee on Armed Services. Defense Policy Panel. *Process and Implications of the Iceland Summit.* 99th Cong., 2d sess. November 21, 24, 25, December 2, 3, 4, 5, and 10.

———. House. 1987a. Committee on Foreign Affairs. Subcommittee on Arms Control, International Security and Science. *Reaction to the Reykjavik Proposals.* 100th Cong., 1st sess. January 29.

———. 1987b. Commission on Security and Cooperation in Europe. *Implementation of Helsinki Accords.* 100th Cong., 1st sess. October 28.

———. Senate. 1988a. Committee on Foreign Relations. *The INF Treaty.* 100th Cong., 2d sess. Jan. 25–28; Feb. 1–5, 16, 18, 19, 22–24; Mar. 3, 14, 16, 17, 22.

————. House. 1988b. Committee on Armed Services. Defense Policy Panel. *General Secretary Mikhail Gorbachev and the Soviet Military: Assessing His Impact and the Potential for Future Changes.* 100th Cong., 2d sess. September 13.

————. House. 1989a. Committee on Armed Services. Defense Policy Panel. *U.S. Defense Budgets in a Changing Threat Environment.* 101st Cong., 1st sess. May 16 and 17.

————. Senate. 1989b. Committee on Foreign Relations. *The Future of U.S.-Soviet Relations.* 101st Cong., 1st sess. April 4, 12, 19, May 3, 15, 18, and June 1 and 20.

————. House. 1990a. Committee on Armed Services. Defense Policy Panel. *Building a Defense That Works for the Post–Cold War World.* 101st Cong., 2d sess. February 22, 28, March 14, 22, 27, and April 25.

————. 1990b. Joint Economic Committee. Technology and National Security Subcommittee. *The Soviet Union Stumbles Badly in 1989.* A paper presented by the CIA and DIA, April 20.

————. Senate. 1991. Select Committee on Intelligence. Nomination of Robert M. Gates to Be Director of Central Intelligence. 102d Cong., 1st sess. October 24.

Vasquez, J. A. 1987. Foreign Policy, Learning and War. In *New Directions in the Study of Foreign Policy,* edited by C. F. Hermann, C. W. Kegley, and J. N. Rosenau. Winchester, MA: Allen & Unwin.

Webster, W. 1990. Statement of the Director of Central Intelligence before the Armed Services Committee. House of Representatives. March 1. Mimeograph.

Weigel, G. 1992. On the Road to Isolationism? *Commentary,* January, 36–42.

Wicker, T. 1990. Cheney vs. Webster. *New York Times,* March 8, A25.

Wildavsky, A. 1966. The Two Presidencies. *Trans-action* 3 (December): 7–14.

————. 1991. *The Beleaguered Presidency.* New Brunswick, NJ: Transaction Publishers.

Will, G. 1989. Europe's Second Reformation. *Newsweek.* November 20, 90.

Wilson, G. C. 1989. Cheney Believes Gorbachev Sincere. *Washington Post,* April 5, A12.

Wines, M. 1990a. Congress Starts Review of U.S. Military Posture. *New York Times,* January 24, A11.

————. 1990b. Webster and Cheney at Odds over Soviet Military Threat. *New York Times,* March 7, A1, A13.

————. 1990c. C.I.A. Accused of Overestimating Soviet Economy. *New York Times,* July 23, A6.

Winik, J. 1989. Restoring Bipartisanship. *Washington Quarterly* 12: 109–22.

————. 1991. The Quest for Bipartisanship: A New Beginning for a New World Order. *Washington Quarterly* 14: 115–30.

Wittkopf, E. R. 1981. The Structure Of Foreign Policy Attitudes: An Alternative View. *Social Science Quarterly* 62: 108–23.

————. 1986. On the Foreign Policy Beliefs of the American People: A Critique and Some Evidence. *International Studies Quarterly* 30: 425–45.

————. 1990. *Faces of Internationalism: Public Opinion and American Foreign Policy.* Durham, NC: Duke University Press.

————. 1994. Faces of Internationalism in a Transitional Environment. *Journal of Conflict Resolution* 38: 376–401.

Wittkopf, E. R., and M. A. Maggiotto. 1983a. Elites and Masses: A Comparative Analysis of Attitudes toward America's World Role. *Journal of Politics* 45: 303–34.

————. 1983b. The Two Faces of Internationalism: Public Attitudes toward American Foreign Policy in the 1970s—and Beyond? *Social Science Quarterly* 64: 288–304.

Wright, R. 1993. Bold Old Vision. *New Republic,* January 25, 22.

Yankelovich, D., and R. Smoke. 1988. America's "New Thinking." *Foreign Affairs* 67: 1–17.

Yergin, D. 1977. *Shattered Peace: The Origins of the Cold War and the National Security State.* Boston: Houghton Mifflin.

Zaller, J. 1992. *The Nature and Origins of Mass Opinion.* New York: Cambridge University Press.

Zeisel, H. 1957. *Say It with Figures.* 4th ed. New York: Harper and Brothers.

Index

Achen, Christopher H., 60, 169n
Adelman, Kenneth L., 20, 161n
Afghanistan, 15, 18–19, 161n
Alden, Edward H., 84–85, 109–10, 175n
Almond, Gabriel A., 50
American Security Council, 14
Anthony, William W., 4
anticommunism, 11, 91, 110
Apple, R. W., Jr., 162n
Arbatov, Georgi, 16
Armacost, Michael, 161n
arms control: Gorbachev's proposals on, 17–18, 19, 30, 161n; hardline and softline assumptions about, 12–13; ideological groups' views on, 23, 103, 175n; and Reagan administration, 15, 18, 19, 20, 21, 160n, 161n. *See also* INF Treaty; SALT II Treaty; SDI; START
Aspin, Les, 19–20, 34
attitude constraint: 6, 169n, 172n; and Americans' Soviet images, 5–6, 9, 49, 54, 55, 56–57, 59, 64, 65–67, 69, 75, 172n; definition of, 4–5, 157n; between foreign policy and domestic domains, 3–4, 6–7, 69, 72–75, 79, 86, 89, 93, 113–14; and panel research design, 5, 133–34. *See also* elite beliefs; enemy images; ideology; values
Augustine, Norman, 37

Babbie, Earl, 131
Baker, James A., III, 32, 35, 161n, 162n, 163n

Baltes, Paul B., 131
Bardes, Barbara: on coherence of mass beliefs, 50, 70; on dimensionality of beliefs, 2, 50, 70; factor analysis results of, 57, 58, 164n, 165n, 168n
Barnet, Richard J., 13, 14, 104, 159n
Bartels, Larry M., 56, 167n
Belarus (Belorussia), 43
belief system: 7; central and peripheral beliefs in, 5–6, 157n; and change, 16, 66, 157n, 160n; definition of, 4–5, 72, 157n; and lessons from history, 1, 157n. *See also* attitude constraint; elite beliefs; ideology; values
belief types: according to views of Soviet Union, 12, 54, 159n; and domestic policy, 172–73n; and MI/CI scheme, 8, 52, 53, 59, 71, 168n; post–Cold War, 91–94, 175n; post-Vietnam, 8, 12–13, 50–53, 93, 159–60n, 166n, 168n. *See also* conservatives; liberals
Belorussia. *See* Belarus
Berlin Wall. *See* Eastern Europe; East Germany
Bernstein, Robert A., 4
Beschloss, Michael: 26, 32, 33, 35, 36, 161n, 162n, 164n; view of, about when Cold War ended, 37
Billingsley, Keith R.: on dimensionality of beliefs, 2, 3, 50, 52, 86; factor analysis results of, 57, 164n, 165–66n, 168n
bipartisanship. *See* consensus